Best Easy Day Hikes
Fort Collins

Help Us Keep This Guide Up to Date

Every effort has been made by the author and editors to make this guide as accurate and useful as possible. However, many things can change after a guide is published—trails are rerouted, regulations change, facilities come under new management, etc.

We would love to hear from you concerning your experiences with this guide and how you feel it could be improved and kept up to date. While we may not be able to respond to all comments and suggestions, we'll take them to heart and we'll also make certain to share them with the author. Please send your comments and suggestions to the following address:

Globe Pequot
Reader Response/Editorial Department
246 Goose Lane, Ste. 200
Guilford, CT 06437

Or you may e-mail us at:

editorial@GlobePequot.com

Thanks for your input, and happy trails!

Best Easy Day Hikes Series

Best Easy Day Hikes Fort Collins

Mary Reed

GUILFORD, CONNECTICUT
HELENA, MONTANA

FALCONGUIDES®

An imprint of Rowman & Littlefield
Falcon and FalconGuides are registered trademarks and Make
Adventure Your Story is a trademark of Rowman & Littlefield

Distributed by NATIONAL BOOK NETWORK

Copyright © 2016 by Rowman & Littlefield

Maps created by Alena Pearce © Rowman & Littlefield

British Library Cataloguing-in-Publication Information Available

Library of Congress Cataloging-in-Publication Data

Names: Reed, Mary T., 1968- author.
Title: Best easy day hikes Fort Collins / Mary Reed.
Description: Guilford, Connecticut : FalconGuides, [2016] | Series:
Best Easy
    Day Hikes Series | "Distributed by NATIONAL BOOK NETWORK"—
T.p. verso.
Identifiers: LCCN 2015050608 (print) | LCCN 2015051410 (ebook)
| ISBN
    9781493019076 (paperback : alk. paper) | ISBN 9781493019083
(e-book)
Subjects: LCSH: Hiking—Colorado—Fort Collins—Guidebooks. | Fort
Collins
    (Colo.)—Guidebooks.
Classification: LCC GV199.42.C6 R45 2016 (print) | LCC GV199.42.
C6 (ebook) |
    DDC 796.5109788/68—dc23
LC record available at http://lccn.loc.gov/2015050608

Contents

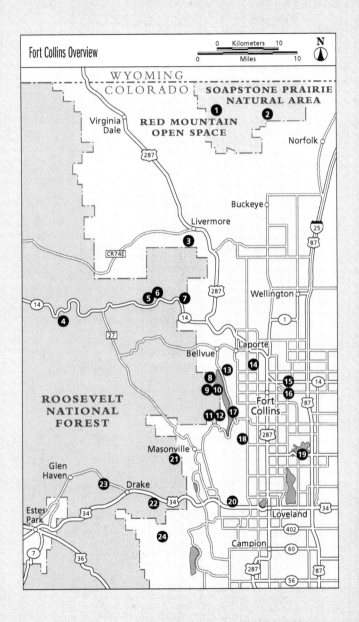

Fort Collins Overview

Kilometers

Miles

N

WYOMING
COLORADO

Virginia
Dale

**SOAPSTONE PRAIRIE
NATURAL AREA**

**RED MOUNTAIN
OPEN SPACE**

Norfolk

Buckeye

Livermore

Wellington

Laporte

Bellvue

Fort
Collins

**ROOSEVELT
NATIONAL
FOREST**

Masonville

Glen
Haven

Drake

Estes
Park

Loveland

Campion

Acknowledgments

Thanks to the friends who hiked with me, schlepped gear, and modeled: David Fanning, Rhonda Hoenigman, and Nicole Wildes.

Thanks to the individuals and organizations who help maintain trails and open space, including the Poudre Wilderness Volunteers (PWV), who work with the Canyon Lakes Ranger District of the US Forest Service to manage and protect wilderness areas. PWV members serve as wilderness rangers and also conduct trail maintenance.

Thanks to the individuals at the public lands agencies who reviewed the entries for hikes on their land: City of Fort Collins Natural Areas Department, Larimer County Natural Resources Department, Roosevelt National Forest, and the Colorado State University Environmental Learning Center.

Thanks to the staff at FalconGuides: Katie Benoit Cardoso, Evan Helmlinger, and Alexandra Singer for their editing and Alena Pearce, who pulled together excellent maps from GPS and source material.

Finally, thanks to my partner, Attila Horvath, who drove, hiked, modeled, and served as first reader of the manuscript.

Introduction

Often ranked as one of the best places in the country to live, Fort Collins is home to Colorado State University, a thriving economy, and—perhaps most important to quality of life—great access to outdoor adventure under 300 days of sun per year. Add thirteen local breweries, including the world-famous New Belgium Brewing, and après-hiking drinks are closer at hand than most trailheads.

Geologically, Fort Collins lies at the foot of the Front Range of the Rocky Mountains. This is where the Great Plains meet the mountains that rise up abruptly, starting at about a mile high—5,280 feet—and topping out at above 14,000 feet. Longs Peak, at 14,259 feet, is a landmark prominently visible from Fort Collins and Loveland and noticeable due to its height—the tallest along the Front Range—and a distinctive notch near the peak visible from the northeast.

Many of the most scenic hikes in and around Fort Collins are along the Cache la Poudre River, or just "the Poudre" as it's known locally. The name is French, and it means to cache or hide the powder—the name supposedly refers to early French trappers hiding their gunpowder along the river. The source of the Poudre is in Rocky Mountain National Park, from where it heads east, carving the Poudre Canyon and then flattening out as it flows through Fort Collins and then Greeley, for a total elevation change of some 7,000 feet. The Poudre was designated by Congress as a National Wild and Scenic River in 1986, and it is certainly both.

Other bodies of water are also important to Fort Collins, for practical as well as recreational uses. Horsetooth Reservoir, a major feature of the Fort Collins landscape, is one of twelve reservoirs that are part of the Colorado–Big

Thompson project, which diverts more than 200,000 acre-feet of water from the west side of the Continental Divide to the eastern side of Colorado, where most of the population lives. Horsetooth Reservoir is surrounded by around 2,000 acres of public land, including more than 50 miles of trails.

Land Management

Both the City of Fort Collins, with its designated natural areas (www.fcgov.com/naturalareas), and Larimer County, with its open spaces (www.larimer.org/naturalresources), had enough forethought to preserve open space for ecological and recreational use. About half the hikes in this book are on city or county land. These agencies offer excellent infrastructure as well as programming, so be sure to check out their websites for seasonal information.

Lory State Park's 2,500 acres lie to the west of Horsetooth Reservoir, and the park is home to 26 miles of trails. Lory State Park and selected county parks and open spaces require day-use fees.

The Roosevelt National Forest covers nearly 1,300 square miles and surrounds most of the hiking areas adjacent to the Poudre River. These hikes are more forested than, and are likely to have more severe elevation gain than, those around town. Additionally, you have access to the backcountry in the national forest. Learn more at www.fs.usda.gov/arp.

The one hike that is not managed by any of these four entities is the Colorado State University Environmental Learning Center, which, by virtue of being owned by a state school, is on state land.

Weather

The Fort Collins area experiences four-season weather, but it seems like you can experience all four seasons in one day at times. Winter tends to be cold (below freezing at night) but sunny and dry. Higher-elevation trails can be snowy and icy, so a pair of Microspikes for your hiking shoes are a good idea in winter. Spring can be cool and wet but also brings with it an array of wildflowers. Summer and fall predictably have the best weather in terms of warm temperatures and sunshine. Late spring through fall are generally the nicest seasons to hike in and around Fort Collins, but any time of year can be quite nice. Just be sure to come prepared in any season with clothing layers, sun protection, and a rain jacket.

Safety and Preparation

In addition to the potential drastic weather changes mentioned above, other potential hazards include injury, wildlife, and noxious plants. In the case that you do twist an ankle, be sure to hike with others and, if you can't, tell someone at home where you are hiking and when you plan to return.

Stinging nettle and poison ivy are two plants that can cause mild to serious skin irritation. Learn to identify these plants and to avoid them—and be sure to keep your dog out of the poison ivy too or you may find yourself with a case later on after you pet your dog.

Among the potentially dangerous critters you might encounter, ticks are most likely. Always do a tick check when you return home from a hike and remove any right away. It takes around 48 hours after a tick attaches to you before infecting you with Lyme disease, so a simple tick check should protect you. However, if you see a bulls-eye rash within a few days, seek medical attention. Rattlesnakes are not uncommon around Fort Collins. Staying on the trail and alert should be enough to prevent an encounter. Mountain lions and bears are uncommonly seen in these parts, but they are here. Again, hiking with a partner or a group is helpful in terms of size and also the noise you will make, which should keep these animals to themselves.

Leave No Trace

A wilderness can accommodate plenty of human use as long as everybody treats it with respect. But a few thoughtless or uninformed visitors can ruin it for everyone who follows. And the need for good manners applies to all wilderness visitors, not just backpackers. Day hikers should also adhere strictly to the "zero impact" principles. The book *Leave No Trace* is a valuable resource for learning more about these principles.

Three FalconGuides Principles of Zero Impact

- Leave with everything you brought with you.
- Leave no sign of your visit.
- Leave the landscape as you found it.

Most of us know better than to litter—in or out of the wilderness. Even the tiniest scrap of paper left along the trail or at the campsite detracts from the pristine character of the Front Range landscape. This means that you should pack out everything, even biodegradable items such as orange peels, which can take years to decompose. It's also a good idea to pick up any trash that less considerate hikers have left behind.

To avoid damaging the trailside soil and plants, stay on the main path. Avoid cutting switchbacks and venturing onto fragile vegetation.

Don't pick up "souvenirs," such as rocks, antlers, feathers, or wildflowers. The next person wants to discover them too, and taking such souvenirs violates park regulations.

Avoid making loud noises that disturb the silence that others may be enjoying. Remember, sound travels easily in the outdoors. Be courteous.

When nature calls, use established outhouse facilities whenever possible. If these are unavailable, bury human waste 6 to 8 inches deep and pack out used toilet paper. This is a good reason to carry a lightweight trowel. Keep wastes at least 300 feet away from any surface water or boggy spots.

Finally, and perhaps most important, strictly follow the pack-it-in/pack-it-out rule. If you carry something into the wilderness, consume it completely or carry it out with you.

Make zero impact—put your ear to the ground in the wilderness and listen carefully. Thousands of people coming behind you will thank you for your courtesy and good sense.

How to Use This Guide

Each hike is described with a map and summary information that delivers the trail's vital statistics, including length, difficulty, fees and permits, park hours, canine compatibility, and trail contacts.

Directions to the trailhead are provided, including the GPS coordinates of the trailhead. Information about what you'll see along the trail, as well as tidbits about natural and cultural history, is provided in the narrative hike description. A detailed route finder (Miles and Directions) sets forth mileages between significant landmarks along the trail.

Getting Around

All of the trails in this guide are within a 45-minute drive of Fort Collins; almost all are within a 30-minute drive of Fort Collins or Loveland. Directions begin from a major intersection in town (College Avenue and a cross street) or near town, such as US 284 and a cross highway or street. Buses (www.ridetransfort.com) and bike paths will get you to a few trailheads on the eastern side of Horsetooth Reservoir, but almost all trailheads require a vehicle to reach them.

Trail Finder

Best Hikes for Easy Access
- 18. Coyote Ridge Trail
- 16. Cottonwood Loop
- 14. North Shields Ponds Trails
- 13. North Loop Trail
- 20. Devil's Backbone Trail Wild Loop
- 15. Riverbend Ponds Trail Loop
- 17. Foothills to Reservoir Loop Trail

Best Hikes for Vistas
- 11. Horsetooth Rock Trail
- 9. Arthur's Rock Trail
- 13. North Loop Trail
- 6. Greyrock Trail
- 2. Towhee Loop
- 23. Crosier Mountain Trail
- 1. Bent Rock Trail
- 18. Coyote Ridge Trail
- 7. Black Powder Trail
- 3. 3 Bar Trail

Best Hikes for Forests
- 22. Foothills Nature Trail
- 4. Kreutzer Nature Trail
- 23. Crosier Mountain Trail
- 24. Shoshone to Besant Point Trail Loop
- 9. Arthur's Rock Trail
- 8. Well Gulch Nature Trail

Best Hikes for Rock Features

11. Horsetooth Rock Trail
9. Arthur's Rock Trail
1. Bent Rock Trail
20. Devil's Backbone Trail Wild Loop
6. Greyrock Trail
10. Shoreline Trail

Best Hikes for Water

12. Horsetooth Falls Trail
5. Hewlett Gulch Trail
10. Shoreline Trail
16. Cottonwood Loop
1. Bent Rock Trail
14. North Shields Ponds Trails
24. Shoshone to Besant Point Trail Loop
19. Cattail Flats Trail
15. Riverbend Ponds Trail Loop

Best Hikes for Wildlife

16. Cottonwood Loop
17. Foothills to Reservoir Loop Trail
19. Cattail Flats Trail
2. Towhee Loop
21. Valley Loop Trail
23. Crosier Mountain Trail
15. Riverbend Ponds Trail Loop

Best Hikes for Wheelchair Access

21. Valley Loop Trail
18. Coyote Ridge Trail
14. North Shields Ponds Trails

15. Riverbend Ponds Trail Loop
19. Cattail Flats Trail

Hikes Easiest to Hardest

19. Cattail Flats Trail
16. Cottonwood Loop
14. North Shields Ponds Trails
17. Foothills to Reservoir Loop Trail
15. Riverbend Ponds Trail Loop
10. Shoreline Trail
 8. Well Gulch Nature Trail
12. Horsetooth Falls Trail
13. North Loop Trail
20. Devil's Backbone Trail Wild Loop
 5. Hewlett Gulch Trail
 4. Kreutzer Nature Trail
 1. Bent Rock Trail
 3. 3 Bar Trail
 7. Black Powder Trail
22. Foothills Nature Trail
 2. Towhee Loop
24. Shoshone to Besant Point Trail Loop
23. Crosier Mountain Trail
21. Valley Loop Trail
18. Coyote Ridge Trail
 9. Arthur's Rock Trail
11. Horsetooth Rock Trail
 6. Greyrock Trail

Map Legend

85	Interstate Highway
34	US Highway
14	State Highway
CR 21	County/Forest Road
	Local Road
	Unpaved Road
	Featured Trail
	Trail
	Boardwalk
	State Boundary
	River/Creek
	Intermittent Stream
	Body of Water
	National Forest/Park
	State/County Park
	Bridge
■	Building/Point of Interest
	Campground
	Cave
	Gate
	Parking
	Peak/Summit
	Picnic Area
	Ranger Station
	Restroom
	Scenic View/Viewpoint
○	Town/City
10	Trailhead
	Water
	Waterfall

1 Bent Rock Trail, Red Mountain Open Space

In what seems to be the middle of nowhere, the Bent Rock Trail isn't just a surprise, it's surprisingly diverse and scenic. Parallel a creek through a small red rock canyon with the namesake bend in the sedimentary rock and then complete a loop in wide-open country.

Distance: 3.4-mile lollipop

Hiking time: About 2 hours

Difficulty: Easy

Trail surface: Rocky dirt trail

Best season: Spring or fall

Other trail users: Hikers-only on the Bent Rock Trail

Canine compatibility: Dogs not permitted

Fees and permits: None

Schedule: Mar 1 through Nov 30. Call ahead or check the website around these dates to find out if there are any extensions.

Maps: USGS Table Mountain; Larimer County Natural Resources Department recreation map

Trail contact: Larimer County Natural Resources Department, (970) 679-4570, www.co.larimer.co.us/parks/red_mountain.cfm

Special considerations: There is no water available at the trailhead so bring your own. Weekday firearms hunting occurs during Oct and Nov.

Finding the trailhead: From CO 1 on the north side of Fort Collins, take CR 1 north 3.7 miles to CR 15. Take a left and continue north on CR 15 for 10 miles to CR 78. Take a left (west) on CR 78 and go 0.9 mile to CR 19. Take a right (north) and drive on the gravel road 1.4 miles to CR 21. Take a left (west) and continue 9.6 miles to the trailhead parking. GPS: N40 57.29' / W105 09.49'

The Hike

Red Mountain Open Space is part of the larger 55,000-acre Mountains to Plains Project, a collaboration among Larimer County—which manages Red Mountain Open Space—the City of Fort Collins, the Nature Conservancy, Legacy Land Trust, and Great Outdoors Colorado (funded by Colorado Lottery earnings). But Red Mountain Open Space is a distinct area within this region.

For starters, pay attention and you'll notice the geologic variety here. Begin by hiking on a wide doubletrack and you won't have to watch your feet. Instead, your eyes will likely be drawn upward to the red—as in red rock sandstone red—hogback ridges. Soon you'll parallel Sand Creek and follow it upstream into a small red rock canyon. On your left you'll see the layer cake of sedimentary rock. Before you exit the canyon, you'll notice the namesake Bent Rock, where the horizontal striations take a sudden downward turn. On the right side of the creek, you'll walk over limestone and notice smaller sandstone cliffs—look upward to see colonies of cliff swallows and their distinctive mud nests.

Also as you exit the short canyon, you'll see to the right why Sand Creek flows so well—water pours out of a culvert coming from an unseen reservoir above. Cross the creek one last time here and head into the open space that dominates this region. You'll hike on a red dirt trail among yucca and mountain mahogany. Look for penstemon and yarrow in spring and summer. You may encounter mule deer, though they are most plentiful in winter when the open space is closed to the public in order to help protect wildlife. Look skyward for raptors that will ordinarily include hawks, but bring your binoculars for a chance sighting of falcons or

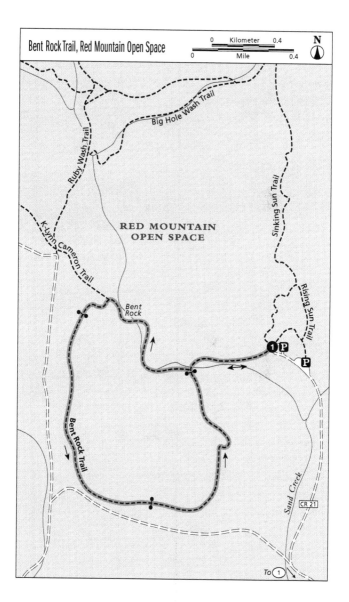

Bent Rock Trail, Red Mountain Open Space

RED MOUNTAIN
OPEN SPACE

Ruby Wash Trail

Big Hole Wash Trail

Sinking Sun Trail

Rising Sun Trail

K-Lynn Cameron Trail

Bent Rock

Bent Rock Trail

Sand Creek

CR 21

To 1

N

Kilometer
0   0.4
Mile
0   0.4

golden eagles—the open space has been home to as many as three nests.

This landscape holds evidence of human inhabitation from more than 10,000 years ago, including projectile points and stone circles. Currently, the area is still used for grazing, so be sure to close the gates behind you when you walk through them on the trail.

Miles and Directions

0.0 Start from the trailhead marked with three large metal signs. Walk west, passing to the left of the picnic shelters.

0.4 Cross Sand Creek on large stepping stones and come to a fork where the Bent Rock Trail loop begins. Take a right to hike it in a counterclockwise direction. Soon enter a red rock canyon.

1.1 After crossing the creek for the third time just downstream from a culvert coming out of an earthen dam, come to a fork. The Bent Rock Trail is marked in both directions, but it is necessary to take the left fork to continue on the loop.

1.2 Pass a gate and be sure to close it behind you.

2.2 Pass another gate and again close it behind you. Soon you will cross an arroyo with wire-reinforced rock cairns. From here, keep looking for cairns to help you stay on the rocky trail.

3.0 Descend and pass through another gate, again closing it behind you.

3.1 Return to the junction where you began the loop. Cross the creek and take a right.

3.4 Arrive back at the trailhead.

2 Towhee Loop, Soapstone Prairie Natural Area

Go on a safari, Colorado-style, at Soapstone Prairie. On any given day, you have a good chance to view pronghorns, coyotes, elk, and—since November 2015—bison. The soundtrack to your hike will undoubtedly be the distinctive, melodious song of the western meadowlark.

Distance: 3.6-mile loop
Hiking time: About 1.5 hours
Difficulty: Easy
Trail surface: Dirt trail with a paved section
Best season: Fall
Other trail users: Hikers-only on the Towhee Trail
Canine compatibility: Dogs not permitted, not even in the car
Fees and permits: None

Schedule: Open dawn to dusk Mar 1 through Nov 30. Check the website or call around these dates to find out if there are extensions.
Maps: USGS Round Butte; City of Fort Collins Natural Areas map
Trail contact: City of Fort Collins Natural Areas, (970) 416-2815, fcgov.com/naturalareas

Finding the trailhead: From the junction of US 287 and CO 1 on the north side of Fort Collins, take CO 1 north 3.7 miles to CR 15. Take a left and continue north on CR 15 13.1 miles to Rawhide Flats Road. Take a right and go past the entrance station to the trailhead parking lot. GPS: N40 58.38' / W105 05.37'

The Hike

Expect delays on your way to and at Soapstone Prairie. No, it won't be due to crowds—this is a great place for solitude compared to Fort Collins's close-by natural areas—it will be because you will likely stop to take a look at wildlife you might more closely associate with Yellowstone National Park than with the city of Fort Collins. A collaboration among the city, Colorado State University, Larimer County, and the US Department of Agriculture brought the bison back to Soapstone Prairie in 2015.

CSU's Animal Reproduction and Biotechnology Laboratory helped to midwife genetically pure Yellowstone bison as a way to rid them of a disease called brucellosis. This paved the way for reintroduction, albeit in a fenced area of 1,000 acres. To learn more, visit www.fcgov.com/naturalareas/bison.php.

Other mammals that will capture your attention include pronghorns, coyotes, and elk. Look skyward for golden eagles and downward for western meadowlarks, jackrabbits, rattlesnakes, and prairie dogs. Though you're unlikely to see them as they are nocturnal, black-footed ferrets—a species once thought to be extinct—were reintroduced to Soapstone in 2014.

The prairie's harsh environment of little water, excessive sun and wind, and bitter winter cold make it rather impressive that these species call this place home. Even more impressive? That humans have called this place home for some 12,000 years. Hike the paved trail 0.4 mile to the Lindenmeier Overlook and learn a bit about a 1930s excavation by the Colorado Museum of Natural History and the Smithsonian Institution that uncovered stone tools dated to 10,000 years old.

After checking out the Lindenmeier site, walk to the Towhee Trail and ascend gently to a ridgetop with sweeping vistas in every direction. Walk through the shrub and

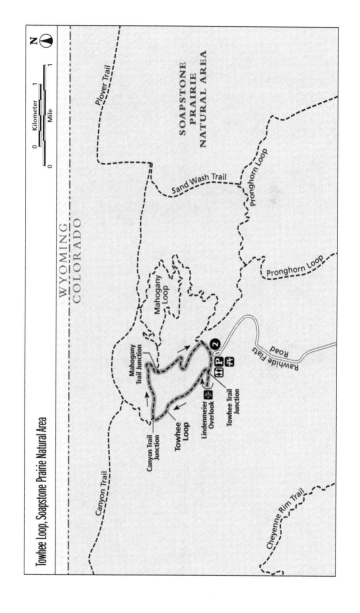

Towhee Loop, Soapstone Prairie Natural Area

grassland dominated by mountain mahogany. In the summer hike in early morning or evening to avoid the harsh sun and to see flowers that include larkspur, bush sunflower, and blanket flower. Descend the ridge and return to where you began.

Miles and Directions

0.0 Start at the paved trail by the pit toilet. Walk west to the trailhead kiosk and then take a right.

0.2 Come to a marked junction with the dirt Towhee Trail. First, stay on the paved trail, taking a switchback to the overlook.

0.4 Arrive at the Lindenmeier Overlook. From here, turn around and return to the junction with the Towhee Loop.

0.6 Arrive at the junction with the Towhee Loop. Take a left and begin the dirt trail.

1.7 Come to a junction with the Canyon Trail on the left, marked with a sign. Continue straight.

2.5 Approach a marked junction with the Mahogany Trail. Take a right to continue on the Towhee Loop.

3.5 Come to the second junction with the Mahogany Trail. Continue straight.

3.6 Arrive back at the trailhead.

3 3 Bar Trail, Eagle's Nest Open Space

"Big sky country" is a phrase associated with Montana, but it applies just as well to Eagle's Nest Open Space in northern Colorado. Hike through this expansive grassland with majestic vistas that change with every step and include distant mountains, mesas, rock outcroppings, and, yes, lots of sky.

Distance: 2.5-mile loop
Hiking time: About 1.5 hours
Difficulty: Easy
Trail surface: Dirt road and trail
Best seasons: Spring and fall
Other trail users: Equestrians
Canine compatibility: Leashed dogs permitted
Fees and permits: None
Schedule: Sunrise to sunset year-round
Maps: USGS Livermore; Larimer County Natural Resources Department recreation map

Trail contact: Larimer County Natural Resources Department, (970) 679-4570, www.co.larimer .co.us/parks/eagles_nest.cfm
Special considerations: There is no water available at the trailhead, and the weather can be quite hot and windy in the summer. Trail closures due to trail conditions occur, so check before heading out.

Finding the trailhead: At the traffic light on the north side of Fort Collins where US 287 turns north, travel 16.8 miles to Red Feather Lakes Road. Take a left (west) and go 0.2 mile to the entrance to Eagle's Nest Open Space on the left (south) side of the road. Drive 1.1 miles to the parking lot and trailhead. GPS: N40 46.58' / W105 12.56'

The Hike

Eagle's Nest Open Space is named after Eagle's Nest Rock, which—you guessed it—gets its name from the golden eagle nests that have reportedly called the rock home since time out of mind. You can almost count on observing raptors any day here, including red-tailed hawks, prairie falcons, and golden eagles. Before heading out for a hike, check the park's website, Facebook page, or Twitter account for any wildlife closures or closures due to especially muddy trails.

The 3 Bar Trail is named after an old cattle brand used in this area that is simply three horizontal bars stacked atop one another, and the trail blaze uses the same image. The adjoining OT Trail is blazed with another old local ranching family cattle brand. And ranching is not simply a thing of the past—be sure to close and lock all gates behind you when you pass through.

Begin a counterclockwise loop with some of the most sweeping vistas of the hike. Make sure to stay on the designated trail and to steer clear of any roads or trails marked "No Public Access." Gently work your way down toward the North Fork of the Poudre River. At the junction where you begin your return on the 3 Bar Trail Loop, you can instead take a right and walk down to the river and back. If you want an even longer hike, you can combine the 3 Bar and OT Trails for a total of 5.2 miles.

Return by walking uphill on the slope below Eagle's Nest Rock, which you can see to the southeast. Look upward for eagles and keep your eyes and ears open for rabbits, deer, coyotes, mountain lions . . . and rattlesnakes. If you get a chance, check out the nearby nineteenth-century Forks general store on US 287, where you can also get prepared food.

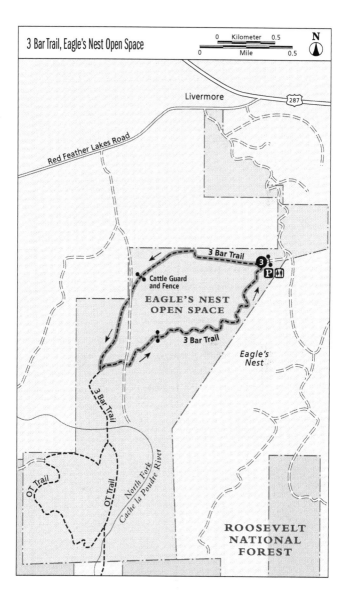

3 Bar Trail, Eagle's Nest Open Space

0   Kilometer   0.5

0   Mile   0.5

N

Livermore

287

Red Feather Lakes Road

3 Bar Trail

3

P

Cattle Guard
and Fence

EAGLE'S NEST
OPEN SPACE

3 Bar Trail

Eagle's
Nest

3 Bar Trail

OT Trail

OT Trail

North Fork
Cache la Poudre River

ROOSEVELT
NATIONAL
FOREST

Miles and Directions

0.0 Start at the gate to the left of the trailhead board. Walk through the gate and latch it behind you. You can take the loop in either direction, but if you head counterclockwise, take a right and start walking downhill on a dirt road.

0.7 The road/trail crosses a cattle guard. You can walk to the left of it through a gate. Again, be sure to lock the gate behind you. Just past the cattle guard, the road forks. Take the left fork.

0.8 The road forks again at a trail post that directs you to take the right fork.

1.2 Come to a four-way intersection. The 3 Bar Trail loop goes to the left. Take the left. (**Option:** You can take a right for a side trip down to the river and back.) The conditions change from dirt road to dirt trail at this point.

1.3 Cross a road and a wash. Continue straight and begin ascending.

1.6 Pass through another gate (and lock it behind you).

2.5 Finish the loop at the trailhead where you began. Don't forget to lock the trailhead gate again.

4 Kreutzer Nature Trail, Roosevelt National Forest

Just 45 minutes from Fort Collins, the trails on Mount McConnel provide more of an alpine feel than most hikes this close to the foothills. Start near the Poudre River in the popular Mountain Park campground and hike partway up Mount McConnel, where you can enjoy a forested hike with views.

Distance: 2.4-mile loop
Hiking time: About 1.5 hours
Difficulty: Easy
Trail surface: Rocky dirt trail
Best season: Summer
Other trail users: Hikers only
Canine compatibility: Leashed dogs permitted
Fees and permits: Parking fee required
Schedule: US Forest Service lands are open 24/7, 365 days a year, but the entrance gate to Mountain Park may be closed due to snow. You can access the trailhead by foot, but pullout parking is limited.
Maps: USGS Poudre Park; Trails Illustrated map 101 (Cache La Poudre/Big Thompson)
Trail contact: Roosevelt National Forest Canyon Lakes Ranger District, (970) 295-6700, www.fs.usda.gov/main/arp
Special consideration: Rifle-hunting season generally falls in Oct–Nov, so you may want to wear blaze orange or avoid the trails during that time.

Finding the trailhead: From the junction where CO 14 and US 287 split (Ted's Place), head west on CO 14 up the Poudre Canyon 23 miles to the entrance to Mountain Park on the left. Cross over a wooden bridge and take a right where the road forks. Park at the trailhead day parking near the pit toilet. GPS: N40 41.01' / W105 27.53'

The Hike

To arrive at the Mount McConnel Trailhead, you are "required" to drive up the winding Poudre Canyon, which gets more attractive with each mile you ascend. By the time you arrive at Mountain Park (the campground is Mountain Park and the trails that begin here are the Mount McConnel and Kreutzer Nature Trails), you're in a forested landscape with the rushing Poudre River cutting a relatively narrow canyon.

As you drive into Mountain Park, cross a wooden vehicle bridge (the trail where you will exit is just to the left on the other side of the bridge) and take a right, entering the day-use area—that is, unless you are camping at the popular Mountain Park campground. Begin at the well-marked trailhead and walk downstream back to the entrance road and cross the road before ascending in earnest. This section of trail is littered with pasqueflower in early spring.

You'll walk by a number of interpretive signs, including one that explains the name of the Kreutzer Nature Trail. It's named after William (Bill) Kreutzer, who was the first forest ranger in the United States, beginning in 1898. He went on to serve in several forests in this region for the next forty-one years, including the Gunnison National Forest and the Battlement Mesa Forest Reserve (now the Grand Mesa Uncompahgre and Gunnison National Forests).

Other interpretive signs explain much of what you should expect to see on this trail. For starters, at a higher elevation you'll see some aspen trees out of the gate, plus ponderosa pines and Douglas firs. Chipmunks and Albert's squirrels are common here, as are many chatty birds like

Steller's jays, mountain chickadees, and woodpeckers. Look for mule deer as well.

As you ascend Mount McConnel, you'll be afforded some overlooks. Arrive at the junction of the Kreutzer Nature Trail (#936) and the Mount McConnel Trail (#992) and take the Kreutzer Trail for a shorter and less steep option. Just after the junction, find a wide, flat rock that makes a good place for a rest and a snack. The trail gets considerably rocky here, which means you'll be looking at your feet in competition with the views of the Wild and Scenic (both officially and unofficially) Poudre River below. You'll notice the remnants of the High Park fire of 2012.

When you arrive at the second junction with the Mount McConnel Trail, you'll see junipers and a seasonal stream cutting down the mountain. Watch your footing, as the soil and rocks can be loose here. Descend as steeply as you ascended back down to the river. The trail comes out at the access road and you'll need to walk along it another 0.2 mile back to the trailhead.

Miles and Directions

0.0   Start at the trailhead kiosk in the day-hike parking area. The trail begins just behind the trailhead sign. Walk in a downstream direction (east). In about 400 feet, the trail forks. Take either fork and cross the campground road, then come to another trail sign. Walk past the sign.

0.3   Come to a T intersection with an interpretive sign. Take a left.

0.5   Arrive at an overlook where the trail switches back to the left.

1.0   Approach a junction where the Kreutzer Interpretive Trail and the Mount McConnel Trail split. Go straight.

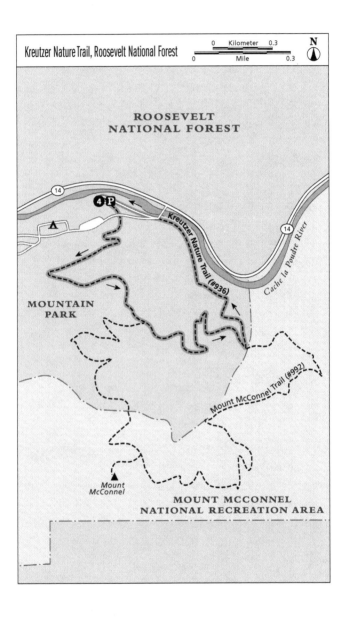

Kreutzer Nature Trail, Roosevelt National Forest

Kilometer
0   0.3
Mile
0   0.3

N

ROOSEVELT
NATIONAL FOREST

14

4 P

Kreutzer Nature Trail (#936)

14

Cache la Poudre River

MOUNTAIN
PARK

Mount McConnel Trail (#992)

Mount
McConnel

MOUNT MCCONNEL
NATIONAL RECREATION AREA

1.6 Come to the second junction where the Mount McConnel Trail and the Kreutzer Interpretive Trail rejoin. Switch back to the left.

2.2 End near the bridge on which you drove across the Poudre River to enter the park. Walk on the paved road back to the trailhead.

2.4 Arrive back at the trailhead.

5 Hewlett Gulch Trail, Roosevelt National Forest

The deservedly popular Hewlett Gulch Trail is a flat path along a riffling creek that you will cross a number of times in a relatively wide and open gulch. Bring your sandals or waterproof boots and enjoy the water, views, flora, and fauna.

Distance: 4.2 miles out and back

Hiking time: About 2 hours

Difficulty: Easy

Trail surface: Dirt trail with stream crossings

Best season: Spring through fall

Other trail users: Mountain bikers, equestrians

Canine compatibility: Controlled dogs permitted

Fees and permits: None

Schedule: US Forest Service lands are open 24/7, 365 days a year

Maps: USGS Poudre Park; Trails Illustrated map 101 (Cache La Poudre/Big Thompson)

Trail contact: Roosevelt National Forest Canyon Lakes Ranger District, (970) 295-6700, www.fs .usda.gov/main/arp

Special considerations: There are a lot of stream crossings; come prepared to make them, especially in the spring, when water can be high. Rifle-hunting season generally falls in Oct–Nov, so you may want to wear blaze orange or avoid the trails during that time.

Finding the trailhead: From the junction of CO 14 and US 287 north of Fort Collins (Ted's Place), drive west on CO 14 up the Poudre Canyon 10.5 miles. Turn right at the marked drive to the trailhead parking. GPS: N40 41.27' / W105 18.35'

The Hike

Hewlett Gulch Trail (#954) is one of the few trails around Fort Collins that follows moving water along its entirety. Better yet, it's a mountain creek that creates a relatively flat gulch—you will gain less than 500 feet in elevation in the 2.1 miles from the trailhead to the turnaround point. During most of the year, the nine or ten creek crossings are easily navigated over stepping stones, but come prepared for high water or slippery rocks and wear either sandals in warm weather or waterproof boots in cold weather. The creek crossings are a great part of the charm of the Hewlett Gulch Trail.

Begin near the junction of the Poudre River and Gordon Creek, which carved out Hewlett Gulch over millennia. Hike upstream in a fairly wide, open, and dry landscape of grasses, shrubs, prickly pear cactus, and the invasive mullein. There is a fair amount of bird activity here, so listen and look for songbirds such as chickadees and woodpeckers, including flickers. Close to the creek you'll walk among cottonwoods, ponderosa pine, and blue spruce. Flowering plants include poppies, blanket flowers, and larkspur.

At about the half-mile point, notice foundations on the left (west) side of the trail, plus a chimney and stovepipe. You'll see more remnants along the trail of the former Poudre Park, a collection of homesteads that were built in the early years of the twentieth century. According to Roosevelt National Forest literature, one of the inhabitants of the former Poudre Park was Horace Huleatt, who around 1870 settled the gulch that came to bear his name (phonetically, anyway). The current hamlet of Poudre Park is located just downstream of Hewlett Gulch.

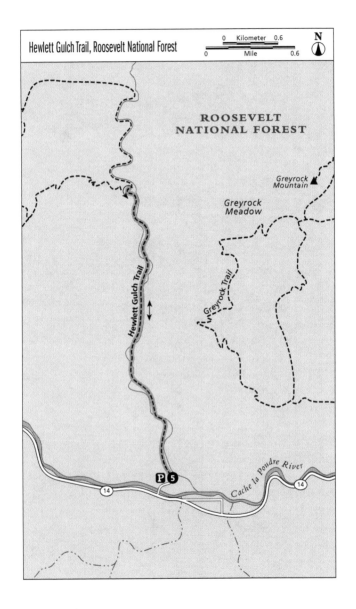

Hewlett Gulch Trail, Roosevelt National Forest

ROOSEVELT
NATIONAL FOREST

Greyrock
Mountain

Greyrock
Meadow

Hewlett Gulch Trail

Greyrock Trail

Cache la Poudre River

14

P 5

14

The trail is very popular among mountain bikers, who have essentially kept open the loop trail that begins toward the north end of the Hewlett Gulch Trail. The suggested turnaround point at mile 2.1 is where the loop begins toward the west. Combining the Hewlett Gulch Trail with the mountain bike loop totals about 8.3 miles.

Miles and Directions

0.0 Start at the trailhead on the north side of the parking lot, near the pit toilet. Walk north.

0.2 Cross the creek twice in quick succession. These are the first of about nine stream crossings.

2.1 Come to a fork with a trail sign for Hewlett Gulch Trail (#954). Turn around here. (**Option:** You can complete the loop and double the length of your hike to about 8.3 miles.)

4.2 Arrive back at the trailhead.

6 Greyrock Trail, Roosevelt National Forest

It might be a stretch to call the Greyrock Trail an easy day hike, but it's not a stretch to call it a classic Fort Collins–area hike. Start at the Poudre River and ascend a mountain to a meadow and skirt the base of this granite massif before descending a verdant gulch.

Distance: 5.8-mile lollipop
Hiking time: 3 to 4 hours
Difficulty: More challenging due to elevation gain and length
Trail surface: Rocky dirt trail
Best season: Late spring to early fall
Other trail users: Hikers only
Canine compatibility: Leashed dogs permitted
Fees and permits: None
Schedule: US Forest Service lands are open 24/7, 365 days a year

Maps: USGS Poudre Park; Trails Illustrated map 101 (Cache La Poudre/Big Thompson)
Trail contact: Roosevelt National Forest Canyon Lakes Ranger District, (970) 295-6700, www.fs .usda.gov/main/arp
Special considerations: The parking lot fills up quite early on weekends; go early or find another trail. Rifle-hunting season generally falls in Oct–Nov, so you may want to wear blaze orange or avoid the trails during that time.

Finding the trailhead: From the junction where CO 14 and US 287 split (Ted's Place), head west on CO 14 up the Poudre Canyon 8.3 miles to the parking lot on the left. After parking, walk down pedestrian stairs and cross the road. Then take the footbridge over the Poudre River to the trailhead kiosk. GPS: N40 41.43' / W105 17.05'

The Hike

The Greyrock Trail is both challenging and satisfying. Come prepared for a good half-day outing so that you don't end up calling Larimer County Search and Rescue as so many others have. Bring plenty of water (there is no potable water at the trailhead), a sun hat (the meadow trail is exposed), and make sure you are fit enough to hike 1,500 to 2,000 vertical feet. Also, make sure you can identify poison ivy. That said, this is one of the best hikes in the region by just about any standard.

From the parking area, cross the road and then cross the Poudre River over a footbridge. The views are already stellar. Walk upstream along the rushing river to a junction of the Greyrock Trail (#946) and the Greyrock Meadows Trail (#947). The Greyrock Trail is the steeper option. Take the Greyrock Meadows Trail, which is largely an open, exposed southern aspect. You'll see blackened snags from the 2012 Hewlett Park and High Park fires. Ascend the mountainside and, before the trail switches back to the east and becomes rocky, peer over a steep drop-off to the west to see Hewlett Gulch below. Once you ascend this first major ridge, the unmistakable Greyrock comes into view.

Approach and then walk along the edge of Greyrock Meadow. If you're doing an overnight, you can camp in Greyrock Meadow. This is also a great wildflower hike. In spring look for pasqueflower, sand lily, then toadflax; in summer look for lupine, miner's candle, and penstemon. The return trail is a steeper downhill and follows a tree-lined gulch.

The Greyrock Trail is a National Recreation Trail. It was built in the 1930s by Civilian Conservation Corps workers as

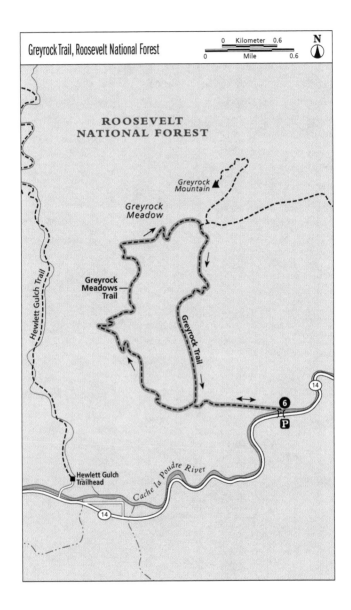

Kilometer

Mile

N

**ROOSEVELT
NATIONAL FOREST**

Greyrock
Mountain

Greyrock
Meadow

Greyrock
Meadows
Trail

Hewlett Gulch Trail

Greyrock Trail

14

6

P

Hewlett Gulch
Trailhead

Cache la Poudre River

14

part of Roosevelt's New Deal. Today, the trail is maintained by the Poudre Wilderness Volunteers, a nonprofit organization with more than 300 volunteers who help the Canyon Lakes Ranger District of the Roosevelt National Forest manage the Poudre Wilderness area through trail restoration and patrols. Learn more at www.poudrewildernessvolunteers.org.

Miles and Directions

0.0 Start from the trailhead kiosk on the north side of the Poudre River. Walk upstream on the trail.

0.6 Come to a junction where the Greyrock Meadows Trail (#947) and the Greyrock Trail (#946) split. Trend left, following the sign for the Greyrock Meadows Trail.

1.8 Ascend to a switchback at a spot that overlooks Hewlett Gulch and then watch carefully to stay on the trail as it becomes rocky.

3.5 Arrive at the junction with the Greyrock Trail, below Greyrock. Take a right and walk toward a bench. (***Option:*** You can continue straight and hike the spur trail to the top of Greyrock. This will require some hands-and-feet scrambling.)

5.2 Return to the original junction where you began your loop. Take a left and return to the trailhead the way you came.

5.8 Arrive back at the trailhead.

7 Black Powder Trail, Gateway Natural Area

Start at the clear, riffling North Fork of the Poudre River and ascend to a mountain meadow so beautiful you'll feel like Maria von Trapp in *The Sound of Music*!

Distance: 1.5-mile lollipop
Hiking time: About 1 hour
Difficulty: Easy but steep
Trail surface: Dirt road and rocky singletrack trail
Best season: Summer
Other trail users: Anglers
Canine compatibility: Leashed dogs permitted

Fees and permits: Day-use fee Mar–Nov
Schedule: Dawn to dusk
Maps: USGS Laporte; Fort Collins Natural Areas map
Trail contact: City of Fort Collins Natural Areas, (970) 416-2815, fcgov.com/naturalareas/finder/gateway

Finding the trailhead: From the junction of US 287 and CO 14 at the mouth of the Poudre Canyon (Ted's Place), turn left (west) on CO 14 and take it up the Poudre Canyon 5.3 miles to Gateway Natural Area on the right. Travel another 0.3 mile from the entrance, passing the ranger residence, and park near the picnic shelters. GPS: N40 42.05' / W105 14.30'

The Hike

The Black Powder Trail is a great outing, top to bottom—or rather, bottom to top. One of the first things you'll notice when you arrive is that hikers are outnumbered by anglers casting for trout. Start by crossing over two bridges, one right after the other. The first crosses the Poudre River and the second crosses the North Fork of the Poudre, just upstream from the confluence of the two. Clear water riffles over a rocky streambed. The Poudre is a designated Wild and Scenic River.

The name of the trail, Black Powder, is presumably a reference to the full name of the Cache la Poudre River. The French *cache la poudre* translates to "hide the powder," referring to gunpowder that early French trappers supposedly buried around here.

The views of the river, rock outcroppings, and tree-dotted mountainsides are lovely. After walking upstream along the river for a few hundred feet, begin ascending the ridge. There are ponderosa pines here, but the farther you look, the more you'll notice the results of the 2012 High Park fire that devastated much of the forest here. The trail ascends fairly steeply, but it switches back enough to make the ascent manageable.

As you near the top of the trail, stop at a tree-studded rocky outcrop and look northwest to see Seaman Reservoir in the near distance and mountains beyond that. Then continue to a plateau and a mountain meadow with a few pines. Walk a loop that takes you close to several steep and long drop-offs (be careful with kids) before returning the way you came.

Miles and Directions

0.0 Start by walking around the gate and crossing two bridges over the North Fork of the Poudre River. In about 250 feet, come to the end of the second bridge and take a left onto the gravel road.

0.2 The Black Powder Trail (signed) forks off of the road to the right. Take the trail and start ascending the ridge.

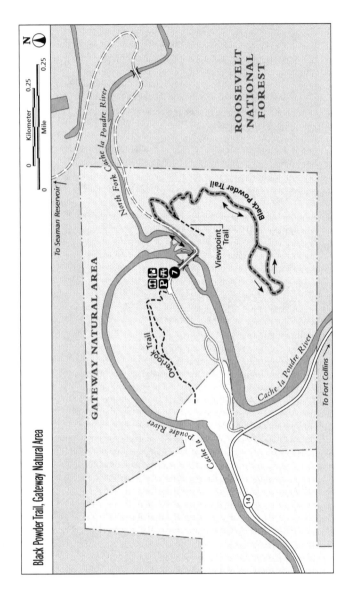

Black Powder Trail, Gateway Natural Area

0.3 Come to a fork. The Viewpoint Trail goes right. Take a left, following the sign that reads "Summit."

0.6 Approach an unsigned, three-way junction. This begins a loop. You can take it either way.

0.9 Arrive back at the spot where you began the loop. Return the way you came.

1.5 Arrive back at the trailhead.

8 Well Gulch Nature Trail to West Valley Trail Loop, Lory State Park

When it comes to wildflowers along the Well Gulch Trail, you name it, you'll see it. Heck, you don't even have to name it—just see and enjoy the amazing display of flowers including lupine, larkspur, wild geranium, spiderwort, and bee balm.

Distance: 1.8-mile lollipop
Hiking time: About 1 hour
Difficulty: Easy
Trail surface: Rocky dirt trail
Best season: May and June
Other trail users: Mountain bikers and equestrians on the West Valley Trail
Canine compatibility: Leashed dogs permitted
Fees and permits: Park entry fee (day or annual)

Schedule: Open dawn to dusk
Maps: USGS Horsetooth Reservoir; Lory State Park trail map; Well Gulch Nature Trail map
Trail contact: Lory State Park, (970) 493-1623, lory.park@state.co.us
Special consideration: Firearms hunting is allowed west of the West Valley Trail in the state park in Oct and Nov.

Finding the trailhead: At the junction (with a stoplight) of CR 54G and North Overland Trail in Laporte, go west on CR 54G 1 mile to Rist Canyon Road. Take a left onto Rist Canyon and go 0.9 mile to CR 23. Take a left (south) and go 1.4 miles to Lodgepole Road. Take a right (west) and continue 1.5 miles to the park entrance on the left. From the visitor center, drive 0.9 mile to a picnic area on the left (east) side of the road. The trailhead is on the west side of the road. GPS: N40 34.42' / W105 10.43'

The Hike

From the open grasslands of the parking lot picnic area and trailhead kiosk, you can't even tell what a cozy, lush trail is ahead of you up Well Gulch. Start by walking across the grassland trail to the west. You have a good chance to see raptors flying above who are looking for prey below.

Enter the gulch and leapfrog over the intermittent stream. The rock walls close in on either side. Take your time on this hikers-only trail to look for wild geranium in the spring and bee balm, spiderwort, and lupine in summer. Cottonwoods grow upstream along the water.

The trail leaves the gulch and ascends partly up the slope. You'll find yourself in a ponderosa pine forest with some Douglas fir (identifiable in part by the "mouse tail" feature of the cone sticking out from the scales) and a few aspen. Walk a fairly flat trail that parallels the slope and then come to another intermittent stream. Start walking downstream, and look and listen for songbirds, including woodpeckers and magpies.

You'll enjoy views to the east of Horsetooth Reservoir and the rocky hogback ridges that parallel the water. Before coming to a second picnic area, come to a junction with the West Valley Trail. Take this trail north back to the first section of the Well Gulch Trail and follow that back to the trailhead.

Miles and Directions

0.0 Start by walking west to the trailhead kiosk and then past it, toward the canyon.

0.1 Come to a footbridge with a junction at each end. Cross the footbridge and then take a right, following the sign for the Well Gulch Trail.

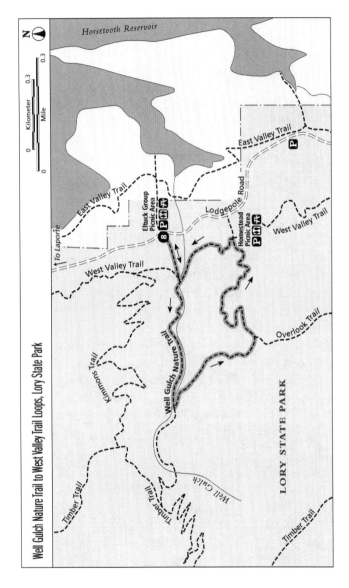

Well Gulch Nature Trail to West Valley Trail Loops, Lory State Park

Horsetooth Reservoir

N

Kilometer
0   0.3

Mile
0   0.3

East Valley Trail

To Laporte

West Valley Trail

Elfruck Group
Picnic Area

8

Lodgepole Road

East Valley Trail

Homestead
Picnic Area

West Valley Trail

Kimmons Trail

Overlook Trail

Well Gulch Nature Trail

Timber Trail

Timber Trail

Well Gulch

Timber Trail

LORY STATE PARK

0.5 Arrive at a three-way junction with a trail sign. Take a left.

0.9 Come to a junction with the Overlook Trail on the right. Continue straight.

1.4 The Well Gulch Trail ends at the junction with the West Valley Trail, just before a picnic area. Take a left to head back to where you began.

1.6 Return to the junction at the footbridge from the start of the hike. Cross back over the footbridge and take a right.

1.8 Arrive back at the trailhead.

⑨ Arthur's Rock Trail, Lory State Park

Arthur's Rock plays second fiddle to Horsetooth Rock, but in reality, the hike to Fort Collins's second-most famous outcropping is an easier day hike and is more varied in terms of landscape features and botany—plus it's (slightly) less crowded than its more famous neighbor to the south.

Distance: 3.4 miles out and back (2.2-mile out-and-back option to overlook only)
Hiking time: About 2 hours
Difficulty: More challenging due to steepness
Trail surface: Rocky dirt trail
Best season: Spring through fall
Other trail users: Hikers only
Canine compatibility: Leashed dogs permitted
Fees and permits: Park entry fee (day or annual)

Schedule: Open dawn to dusk
Maps: USGS Horsetooth Reservoir; Lory State Park trail map; Well Gulch Nature Trail map
Trail contact: Lory State Park, (970) 493-1623, lory.park@state .co.us
Special consideration: Firearms hunting is allowed west of the West Valley Trail in the state park in Oct and Nov.

Finding the trailhead: At the junction (with a stoplight) of CR 54G and North Overland Trail in Laporte, go west on CR 54G 1 mile to Rist Canyon Road. Take a left onto Rist Canyon and go 0.9 mile to CR 23. Take a left (south) and go 1.4 miles to Lodgepole Road. Take a right (west) and continue 1.5 miles to the park entrance on the left. From the visitor center, drive 2.1 miles to the end of the road and the trailhead parking for Arthur's Rock. GPS: N40 33.52' / W105 10.29'

The Hike

You can see the granite massif that is Arthur's Rock from the trailhead. The views change with every step as your goal gets closer and closer. Begin by walking into Arthur's Rock Gulch, where the scenery quickly morphs from open grassland to ponderosa pine forest. You lose sight of Arthur's Rock in the gulch, but you'll want to watch your step anyway, as several sections of the trail have steep drop-offs.

Continue ascending (the entire trail is an ascent) to views again of Arthur's Rock to the northwest and then a mountain meadow. Tall grasses dominate the flora of the meadow. There are plenty of wildflowers along the Arthur's Rock Trail. The showiest include larkspur, penstemon, lupine, and wild sunflower. Plenty of animals call this area home as well, including Albert's squirrels, wild turkeys, and mule deer.

Walk through the meadow and enter the forest again. As the trail gets nearer to Arthur's Rock, it also gets rockier. There are side trails used by rock climbers. As you approach the base of the rock, there is an eastern overlook. You could stop here and turn around for a 2.2-mile option. Continuing up, follow the base of the rock west and then hike up and around the western side of it. Only the very last section of trail, less than a couple hundred feet, is really steep and rocky—you'll likely use both hands and feet to make it to the top, but it is not exposed.

The hike is challenging, and the reward of making it to your destination is worth it. End atop the 6,780-foot Arthur's Rock, which was named after an early settler and affords views of Horsetooth Reservoir and Fort Collins to the east. Don't forget to pack a lunch—find a comfortable spot on

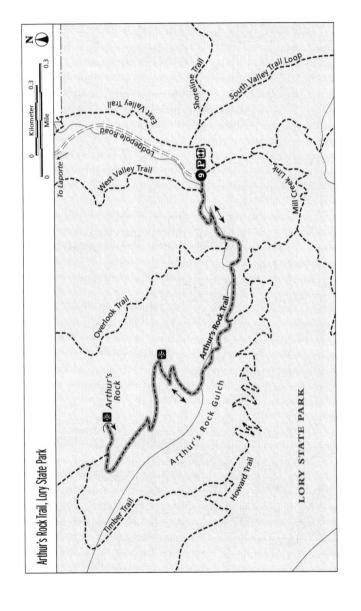

Arthur's Rock Trail, Lory State Park

N

Kilometer 0.3
Mile 0.3

To Laporte

West Valley Trail

East Valley Trail

Lodgepole Road

Shoreline Trail

South Valley Trail Loop

P
9

Mill Creek Link

Overlook Trail

Arthur's Rock

Arthur's Rock Trail

Arthur's Rock Gulch

Timber Trail

Howard Trail

LORY STATE PARK

a boulder in the shade of a ponderosa pine and enjoy your reward before heading back down.

Miles and Directions

0.0   Start at the red-roofed trailhead kiosk on the west side of the parking lot. As you face the kiosk, go right and walk toward the gulch. In about 250 feet, cross a footbridge and come to the junction with the West Valley Trail (marked). Take a left.

0.3   Come to a fork with the Overlook Trail. Take the left fork.

0.6   Arrive at the junction with the Mill Creek Link Trail. Take a right.

0.9   Pass a bouldering access trail on the left. Continue straight.

1.1   Come to a junction with a spur to the scenic overlook. The Arthur's Rock Trail switches back here. (***Option:*** For a shorter hike, you can check out the overlook and return from here for a 2.2-mile out-and-back.)

1.6   Arrive at a junction with the Howard and Timber Trails to the left. Continue straight.

1.7   Arrive at the top of Arthur's Rock. After enjoying a rest or lunch here, return the way you came.

3.4   Arrive back at the trailhead.

10 Shoreline Trail, Lory State Park

Start in grasslands and walk through a break in the red-rocked hogback ridge before descending to the shores of Horsetooth Reservoir on this hike that stands in contrast to most in Lory State Park.

Distance: 1.4 miles out and back
Hiking time: About 45 minutes
Difficulty: Easy
Trail surface: Rocky dirt trail
Best season: Spring or fall
Other trail users: Equestrians, mountain bikers
Canine compatibility: Leashed dogs permitted
Fees and permits: Park entry fee (day or annual)

Schedule: Open dawn to dusk
Maps: USGS Horsetooth Reservoir; Lory State Park trail map; Well Gulch Nature Trail map
Trail contact: Lory State Park, (970) 493-1623, lory.park@state.co.us
Special consideration: Firearms hunting is allowed west of the West Valley Trail in the state park in Oct and Nov.

Finding the trailhead: At the junction (with a stoplight) of CR 54G and North Overland Trail in Laporte, go west on CR 54G 1 mile to Rist Canyon Road. Take a left onto Rist Canyon and go 0.9 mile to CR 23. Take a left (south) and go 1.4 miles to Lodgepole Road. Take a right (west) and continue 1.5 miles to the park entrance on the left. From the visitor center, drive 2 miles to the West Valley and Shoreline Trails parking on the left. GPS: N40 34.03' / W105 10.25'

The Hike

Lory State Park offers many hiking options: Arthur's Rock rises to the west, Horsetooth Reservoir lies to the east, and foothill grasslands stretch north and south. It can be hard to decide which way to start walking, but that's a good problem to have.

The Shoreline Trail offers wildlife viewing, with raptors soaring above and deer grazing the meadow. Look for wildflowers among the grasses, from yuccas in the springtime to asters in the fall.

The trail also allows you to get up close and personal with one of the red rock sandstone hogback ridges that surround Horsetooth Reservoir. This Lyons Sandstone was formed some 300 million years ago, and it is an especially hard type of sandstone. This, combined with its attractive color, has long made it a favored material for construction, landscape, and art projects large and small—you can see examples of its use in the Engineering II building on the Colorado State University campus and (a bit farther afield) a snaking wall installation by famed artist Andy Goldsworthy at the Aspen Institute.

After hiking through the hogback ridge, the trail begins a gentle descent to Horsetooth Reservoir. The reservoir was built in 1949 by the US Bureau of Reclamation as part of the greater Colorado–Big Thompson Project designed to provide water from the mountains to the Front Range. Not one but four earthen dams contain the water that is Horsetooth Reservoir. As you approach the shore, there is a wide grassy area that's good for a picnic (bring a blanket) and surrounded by mature cottonwood trees. This is a good spot to stop for lunch before returning uphill back to where you began.

Miles and Directions

0.0 Start at the red-roofed trailhead kiosk. Facing the trailhead sign, take a left and walk east toward Horsetooth Reservoir.

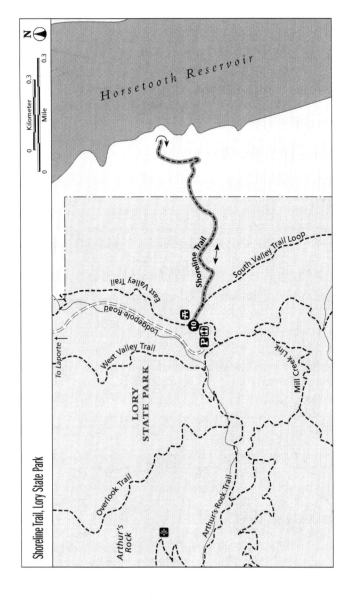

Shoreline Trail, Lory State Park

Horsetooth Reservoir

N

Kilometer   0.3
0
Mile   0.3
0

LORY
STATE
PARK

Shoreline Trail

South Valley Trail Loop

East Valley Trail

Lodgepole Road

West Valley Trail

To Laporte

Mill Creek Link

Overlook Trail

Arthur's Rock

Arthur's Rock Trail

In about 350 feet, come to a fork with a trail sign. Take the left fork to continue on the Shoreline Trail.

0.3 Pass the hogback ridge and the reservoir comes into view. After that, arrive at a fork. Take a left to stay on the main trail.

0.6 Come to another fork. Take either fork as the two trails rejoin in less than 200 feet. At that point, continue descending toward the water.

0.7 End at the shoreline of Horsetooth Reservoir. Return the way you came.

1.4 Arrive back at the trailhead.

11 Horsetooth Rock Trail, Horsetooth Mountain Open Space

Hiking in Fort Collins and not paying a trip to Horsetooth Rock is like being in Paris and not bothering with the Eiffel Tower. It's the very icon of the city, so strap on your boots, walk to the top of Horsetooth Mountain, and make a final scramble atop the granite rock that resembles, well, a horse's tooth.

Distance: 5.0 miles out and back

Hiking time: 2.5 to 3 hours

Difficulty: More difficult, due to length and elevation gain

Trail surface: Dirt trail

Best season: Late spring through fall

Other trail users: Hikers-only on the Horsetooth Rock Trail

Canine compatibility: Leashed dogs permitted

Fees and permits: Daily entrance permit required

Schedule: Horsetooth Mountain trailhead is open 24/7

Maps: USGS Horsetooth Reservoir; Horsetooth Mountain Open Space trail brochure

Trail contact: Horsetooth Mountain Open Space, (970) 498-7000, www.co.larimer.co.us/parks/htmp.cfm

Special consideration: The parking lot fills quickly on weekends, so go early or find another place to hike. Check the parking lot webcam on the Horsetooth Mountain Open Space website.

Finding the trailhead: From US 287 and Harmony Road in Fort Collins, take West Harmony Road (CR 38E) 8.7 miles to the park entrance. Turn right into the entrance. GPS: N40 31.26' / W105 10.51'

The Hike

Paris has the Eiffel Tower, New York has the Statue of Liberty, and Fort Collins has Horsetooth Rock. That's more than just T-shirt wisdom: Horsetooth Rock is the most iconic landscape feature of Fort Collins, and Horsetooth Mountain Open Space is wildly popular among the populace. So popular, in fact, that you should plan to hit the trails on a weekday or arrive quite early on a weekend.

Beginning at around 5,800 feet in elevation, the trail is in a wide-open landscape of grasses and shrubs, including wild plum that blooms profusely in the spring. Look to the southeast to see Longs Peak and the other high mountains in Rocky Mountain National Park. As the Horsetooth Rock and Horsetooth Falls Trails diverge, begin ascending more earnestly. Soon you'll encounter a more forested landscape with ponderosa pine and juniper dominating the landscape. Flowers include pasqueflower, penstemon, lupine, butter-and-eggs, spiderwort, and salsify.

You may encounter Albert's squirrels, coyotes, deer, and other wildlife. Be sure to leave them alone for their own safety and health as well as yours. The higher you ascend, the farther you will be able to see to Fort Collins and beyond to the east. At about mile 1.9 you will see Horsetooth Rock for the first time since your drive to the trailhead. This time it's considerably closer.

Horsetooth Rock is the most recent name given to this distinctive outcropping. There are stories floating around about different old legends surrounding the rock. One refers to a Chief Maununmoku who cleaved an evil giant's heart, thus creating the cleft in Horsetooth Rock. The trail names are reminiscent of the recent history of this land. Families that had homesteads here included the Soderbergs, Wathens, and Culvers. In fact, much of Horsetooth Mountain Park was purchased from the Soderberg family, some as recently as the 1980s.

As you arrive at the top of Horsetooth Mountain, to the north of Horsetooth Rock, you can see the high mountains again to the west. However, to gain a 360-degree view, you'll have to make the final 75-foot push to the summit of Horsetooth Rock, which requires hands-and-feet climbing. Make sure you are comfortable with climbing up—and down—in this fashion before ascending to the top. The spacious peak, at 7,200 feet in elevation, is a great place to have lunch before returning the way you came.

Miles and Directions

0.0 Start at the trailhead kiosk located on the north side of the parking lot. The Horsetooth Rock Trail leads right from the trailhead kiosk and is marked with a sign.

0.3 Arrive at a marked fork with the Horsetooth Falls Trail. Take the left fork to stay on the Horsetooth Rock Trail.

0.6 The South Ridge Trail joins from the left. Continue straight.

0.7 The South Ridge Trail goes off to the left. Again, continue straight.

0.9 Come to a three-way marked junction. Take a left to continue on the Horsetooth Rock Trail.

1.7 Arrive at a five-way junction, again marked. Continue straight, following the sign that reads "Foot Travel Only."

1.9 Come to a fork with an unmarked trail on the left. Take the right fork. In another 100 feet, come to another fork. You will see Horsetooth Rock. Take another right. Then in another 100 feet, a trail comes in from the left. Continue straight.

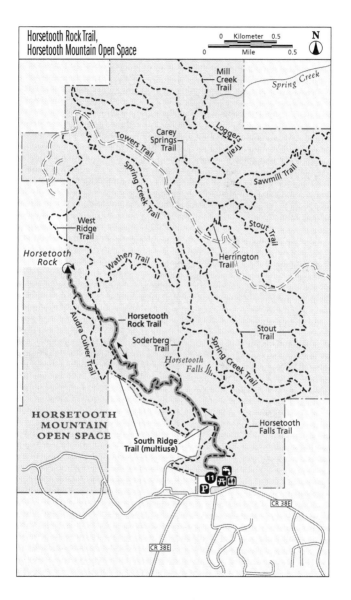

Horsetooth Rock Trail,
Horsetooth Mountain Open Space

Kilometer
Mile

N

Mill
Creek
Trail

Spring Creek

Loggers Trail

Towers Trail

Carey Springs
Trail

Sawmill Trail

Spring Creek Trail

West
Ridge
Trail

Stout Trail

*Horsetooth
Rock*

Wathen Trail

Herrington
Trail

Horsetooth
Rock Trail

Soderberg
Trail

Stout
Trail

*Horsetooth
Falls*

Audra Culver Trail

Spring Creek Trail

HORSETOOTH
MOUNTAIN
OPEN SPACE

South Ridge
Trail (multiuse)

Horsetooth
Falls Trail

11

P

CR 38E

CR 38E

2.0 Approach a junction with the Wathen Trail on the right. Continue straight.

2.1 Come to a sign for Horsetooth Rock, which now leads up a rocky surface.

2.2 Arrive at the junction with the Audra Culver Trail on the left. Take a right.

2.4 Hike to the base of Horsetooth Rock. You can see Longs Peak and the other mountains to the east. The rest is a hands-and-feet scramble to the top of the rock.

2.5 Make it to the top of Horsetooth Rock and enjoy the 360-degree view. Return the way you came.

5.0 Arrive back at the trailhead.

12 Horsetooth Falls Trail, Horsetooth Mountain Open Space

The hike to Horsetooth Falls is an attractive alternative to hiking all the way to the top of Horsetooth Rock, which is not the easiest of easy day hikes. Any time is a nice time to hike to the falls, but plan it after a rain or snowmelt to find the cascade running full.

Distance: 2.4 miles out and back

Hiking time: About 1 hour

Difficulty: Easy

Trail surface: Dirt trail

Best season: Spring, especially after rain or snowmelt

Other trail users: Equestrians, mountain bikers

Canine compatibility: Leashed dogs permitted

Fees and permits: Daily (or yearly) entrance permit required

Schedule: Horsetooth Mountain trailhead is open 24/7

Maps: USGS Horsetooth Reservoir; Horsetooth Mountain Open Space trail brochure

Trail contact: Horsetooth Mountain Open Space, (970) 498-7000, www.co.larimer.co.us/parks/htmp.cfm

Special consideration: The parking lot fills quickly on weekends, so go early or find another place to hike. Check the parking lot webcam on the Horsetooth Mountain Open Space website.

Finding the trailhead: From US 287 and Harmony Road in Fort Collins, take West Harmony Road (CR 38E) 8.7 miles to the park entrance. Turn right into the entrance. GPS: N40 31.26' / W105 10.51'

The Hike

Sometimes the beaten path is beaten for a reason. Case in point: the easy and rewarding hike to Horsetooth Falls. Begin the trail on the north end of the parking lot, marked with a trailhead kiosk and trailhead sign. Start ascending right away in the open foothills landscape of grasses, yucca, and wild plum. The trail is wide and smooth.

Look southwest and you can see the notched Longs Peak and other peaks of Rocky Mountain National Park on the horizon. To the east is Horsetooth Reservoir and to the west is Horsetooth Rock. Bring a sun hat for this trail, as most of it is in the open grass and shrub land.

After the Horsetooth Falls and Horsetooth Rock Trails diverge, continue on the relatively flat Horsetooth Falls Trail. As it enters the Spring Creek Canyon, note how the landscape changes—more trees come into view, and the trail becomes narrower and rockier. Flowers include pasque-flower in the spring and miner's candle and larkspur in the summer.

Walk over Spring Creek on a footbridge before a brief ascent on the other side. Soon you will be able to hear the falls before seeing them. Pass a trail that takes you to the top of the falls (or don't pass it and hike to the top if the spirit moves you) and arrive at your destination. Horsetooth Falls cascade over a large rock wall and into a pool. It's a lovely and cool spot and even has a bench to sit on (if no one has beaten you to it). Bring a lunch and hang out for a while before returning the way you came.

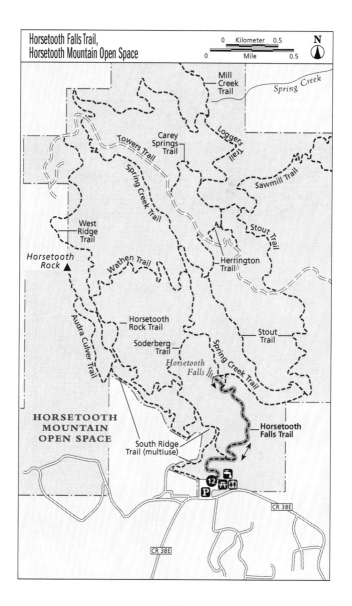

Horsetooth Falls Trail,
Horsetooth Mountain Open Space

0   Kilometer   0.5

0   Mile   0.5

N

Mill Creek Trail

Spring Creek

Loggers Trail

Towers Trail

Carey Springs Trail

Sawmill Trail

Spring Creek Trail

Stout Trail

West Ridge Trail

Herrington Trail

Horsetooth Rock

Wathen Trail

Horsetooth Rock Trail

Stout Trail

Soderberg Trail

Horsetooth Falls

Spring Creek Trail

Audra Culver Trail

HORSETOOTH MOUNTAIN OPEN SPACE

South Ridge Trail (multiuse)

Horsetooth Falls Trail

12

P

CR 38E

CR 38E

Miles and Directions

0.0 Start at the trailhead kiosk located on the north side of the parking lot. The Horsetooth Falls Trail leaves right from the trailhead kiosk and is marked with a sign.

0.3 Come to a fork. Take the right fork for the signed Horsetooth Falls Trail (left is Horsetooth Rock Trail).

0.9 Cross a footbridge and then climb steps that wind back around toward the creek. Soon you will hear the falls.

1.1 Come to a junction with the Top of Falls and Spring Creek Trails on the right. Continue straight.

1.2 Arrive at Horsetooth Falls. After hanging out and enjoying the falls, return the way you came.

2.4 Arrive back at the trailhead.

13 North Loop Trail, Reservoir Ridge Natural Area

This otherwise-typical foothills hike affords views to the west of Horsetooth Reservoir, to the east overlooking Fort Collins, and north into Wyoming.

Distance: 1.4-mile lollipop
Hiking time: About 1 hour
Difficulty: Easy
Trail surface: Rocky dirt trail
Best season: Spring through fall
Other trail users: Mountain bikers, equestrians
Canine compatibility: Leashed dogs permitted
Fees and permits: None
Schedule: 5 a.m. to 11 p.m. daily

Maps: USGS Horsetooth Reservoir; Fort Collins Natural Areas map
Trail contact: City of Fort Collins Natural Areas, (970) 416-2815, fcgov.com/naturalareas
Special considerations: There is no water at the trailhead, so bring your own. Check for trail closures due to muddy conditions at www .fcgov.com/naturalareas/status .php or #FCTrails on Twitter.

Finding the trailhead: From CR 54G on the northwest side of Fort Collins, travel west on Rist Canyon Road 0.9 mile to North CR 23. Turn south (left) and go 1.8 miles to the parking lot on the left (east) side of the road. GPS: N40 36.13' / W105 10.15'

The Hike

The northern terminus of the 9.6-mile Foothills Trail is located in Reservoir Ridge, and this small loop gives you a taste of that trail. Begin by hiking up Reservoir Ridge, which, in fact, is a ridge that serves as the eastern rim of

Horsetooth Reservoir. Expect to see other hikers, mountain bikers, and equestrians on this close-to-town trail.

This area is part of the Dakota Ridge, which refers to the entire length of the first ridgeline along the Front Range between the high plains and the Rocky Mountains. Much of this ridgeline has the classic hogback form with a hard layer of Dakota Sandstone lining the very top of the ridge.

Much of the open landscape is dominated by grasses and the mountain mahogany shrub. The trail is quite rocky, so watch your step, but don't forget to stop and look around. The first views are to the southwest and include Horsetooth Reservoir and Arthur's Rock in Lory State Park on the other side of the water.

As the trail continues around its northern bend, note the presence of juniper and ponderosa pine. Views to the north include long cliff lines and the plains all the way to Wyoming. As you continue walking to the east side of the loop, get an expansive look at the city of Fort Collins. Soon you will join the Foothills Trail briefly before finishing the loop where you started.

Miles and Directions

0.0 Start at the trailhead kiosk. Walk uphill on the trail.

0.2 Come to a junction. Trend left.

0.3 Come to a fork with the Foothills Trail. Take a left and begin the loop, going clockwise.

0.5 Pass the old trail on the right, which is closed for rehabilitation. Continue straight.

0.8 Come to a fork. This is another junction with the Foothills Trail. Take the right fork.

1.0 Come to a T intersection. The Foothills Trail goes left. Take a right to complete the North Loop Trail.

North Loop Trail, Reservoir Ridge Natural Area

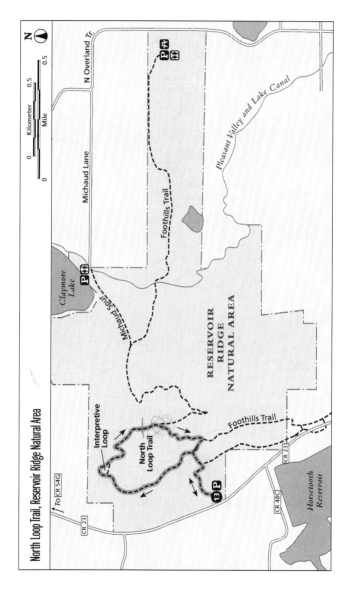

1.1 Return to the junction where you began the loop. Take a left and return to the trailhead the way you came.

1.4 Arrive back at the trailhead.

14 North Shields Ponds Trails, North Shields Ponds Natural Area

Walk around these neighborhood ponds and along the Poudre River while taking in views of the mountains to the west and the watershed restoration efforts conducted here in 2014–2015.

Distance: 1.6-mile loop
Hiking time: About 45 minutes
Difficulty: Easy
Trail surface: Dirt road and trail
Best season: Year-round
Other trail users: Equestrians, anglers
Canine compatibility: Leashed dogs permitted

Fees and permits: None
Schedule: 5 a.m. to 11 p.m. daily
Maps: USGS Fort Collins; City of Fort Collins Natural Areas map
Trail contact: City of Fort Collins Natural Areas, (970) 416-2815, fcgov.com/naturalareas/finder/nshieldspond

Finding the trailhead: From North College Avenue (US 287) and LaPorte Avenue, travel west on LaPorte 0.9 mile to North Shields Street. Go 1.1 miles on North Shields. Cross the Poudre River and enter the trailhead parking lot on the left (west) side of the road. GPS: N40 36.20' / W105 05.46'

The Hike

The North Shields neighborhood still has the feel of the rural area it once was. There's a good chance you'll see people fishing when you arrive, and as you hike around the north side of the ponds, suburban homes give way to ranchettes where horse pastures abut the trail.

Begin a counterclockwise loop by walking along the edge of North Shields Street to gain the north side of the eastern pond. You'll be hiking on a dirt road with the pond to your south and neighborhood homes and access trails to your north. The pond is choked with cattails, so look for water-loving birds, such as red-winged blackbirds.

Soon you'll come to the end of the first little pond—you could circumnavigate it by taking a left to continue around it. But continue instead in a northerly direction, and pass the horses on your right while the second, larger pond is on your left. Greyrock Mountain is in your view near the horizon to the northwest, and Arthur's Rock in Lory State Park is closer to the southwest.

As you approach the Poudre River, the path turns from a dirt road to a foot trail. Walk between the pond and the river for the rest of your journey. Look for river birds such as kingfishers. You'll be heading downstream, and soon you'll see a lot of planted trees and shrubs as well as freshly turned dirt. But this is not from the floods of 2013. Rather, it's from a water-restoration project in which a dam-like diversion structure was dismantled in 2014.

Miles and Directions

0.0 Start from the trailhead kiosk. Walk to the right of the kiosk on a boardwalk that leads to a fishing platform. Before the platform take a right and step onto a crushed-gravel trail. Take this trail back to Shields Street and cross north over the river alongside the road. Take a left on the other side of the bridge and begin walking west on a dirt road.

0.3 Approach an open area that resembles a parking lot. To the left is a trail that leads back around the first pond. Trend right until the path resembles a road again, and begin walking around the second pond.

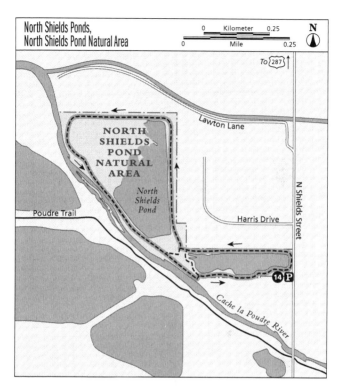

0.9 As the road turns into a trail, start heading south and begin paralleling the Poudre River downstream.

1.2 In the washed-out floodplain, trails start to braid. The main trail sticks close to the river's edge, continuing downstream.

1.3 Come to a junction with the trail that circumnavigates the first pond. Continue straight.

1.5 The trail forks; a sign points horses right. Take the left fork.

1.6 Arrive back at the trailhead.

15 Riverbend Ponds Trail Loop, Riverbend Ponds Natural Area

Once a gravel mine, Riverbend Ponds is now a neighborhood natural area where you are guaranteed to see a variety of birds and other water-loving wildlife while you hike.

Distance: 2.4-mile loop
Hiking time: About 1 hour
Difficulty: Easy
Trail surface: Dirt road and singletrack trail
Best seasons: Spring and fall
Other trail users: Mountain bikers, equestrians
Canine compatibility: Leashed dogs permitted

Fees and permits: None
Schedule: 5 a.m. to 11 p.m. daily
Maps: USGS Loveland; Fort Collins Natural Areas map
Trail contact: City of Fort Collins Natural Areas, (970) 416-2815, fcgov.com/naturalareas/finder/riverbend

Finding the trailhead: From the junction of College Avenue and Prospect Road in Fort Collins, head east on East Prospect Road 2.8 miles to the parking lot on the left (north) side of the road. GPS: N40 34.04' / W105 01.22'

The Hike

The land that is now Riverbend Ponds Natural Area was mined for gravel from the 1950s through the 1970s. The seven mining pits filled, over time, with water. Then the plants and animals moved in. Then the City of Fort Collins purchased the land and turned it into a public natural area.

This hike on unnamed trails takes you around several ponds that—you guessed it—are located next to a southward bend in the Poudre River. Walk to your first junction in front of the Big Pond Trail and begin a clockwise loop. Listen for the loud, trilling call of the red-winged blackbird, which you'll find perched on the cattails along the edges of the ponds. They are among some 200 species of birds that live here full-time or part of the year. Some of the biggest and most impressive are great blue herons, ospreys, and cormorants. Dawn and dusk are great times to hike in order to observe active wildlife, avian and otherwise. Foxes are commonly seen here, as are mule deer.

Rabbitbrush is the dominant shrub and it attracts butterflies when in bloom. Lining the ponds and the Poudre River are towering cottonwood trees.

As you pass one, two, three ponds and the northern trailhead, you'll take a right and walk along a spit of land between Turtle Pond on the west and Trout Pond on the east. They are appropriately named—look on logs poking out of the ponds for snapping turtles sunning themselves. You'll see plenty of anglers, as these ponds are stocked by Colorado Parks and Wildlife mostly with bass, bluegill, and catfish (trout actually prefer cooler water). Then approach another junction between three ponds and take a left to walk over a boardwalk before hitting dry land again, completing the loop, and returning to the trailhead.

Miles and Directions

- **0.0** Start at the trailhead kiosk at the far end of the parking lot, past the gate.
- **0.2** Come to a T intersection at Big Pond. Take a left to begin a clockwise loop.

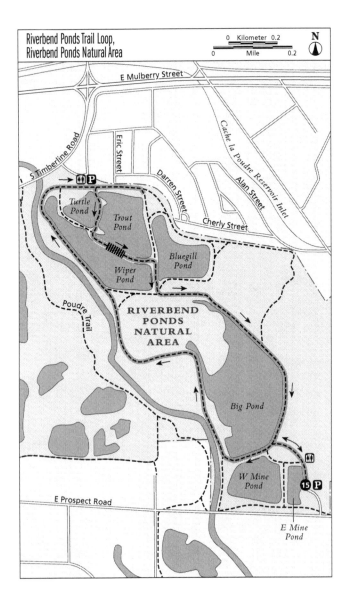

Riverbend Ponds Trail Loop,
Riverbend Ponds Natural Area

0   Kilometer   0.2

0   Mile   0.2

N

E Mulberry Street

S Timberline Road

Eric Street

Darren Street

Cache la Poudre Reservoir Inlet

Alan Street

Cherly Street

Turtle Pond

Trout Pond

Wiper Pond

Bluegill Pond

Poudre Trail

RIVERBEND
PONDS
NATURAL
AREA

Big Pond

W Mine Pond

E Prospect Road

15

E Mine Pond

0.7 Still walking on the road, pass a side trail on the right to a bench. This meets up with the road again.

0.9 Arrive at a T intersection. Take a left. (***Option:*** Take a right and walk back along Big Pond for an approximately 1.6-mile loop.)

1.2 The dirt road curves east as you approach the northern parking lot and pass a side trail on the right. Pass the northern trailhead kiosk on your left, and arrive at a junction with a trail between Trout and Turtle Ponds on your right. Take a right here and walk along the narrow spit of land between the two ponds.

1.3 Come to a three-way intersection where Trout and Turtle Ponds meet Wiper Pond. Take a left.

1.4 Cross a boardwalk over Wiper Pond.

1.5 Come to a T intersection with Bluegill Pond ahead. Take a right.

1.6 Arrive at another T intersection with Big Pond in front of you. Take a left and walk along the edge of Big Pond to where you began.

1.7 Come to another T intersection. Take a right, continuing clockwise.

2.2 Return to the junction where you started the loop. Take a left and walk toward the pit toilet.

2.4 Arrive back at the trailhead.

16 Cottonwood Loop, Colorado State University Environmental Learning Center

This is a great place to be a student of nature. Enjoy edge habitats of grasslands, cottonwoods, and the Poudre River. Listen and look for birds and enjoy walking over a suspension footbridge.

Distance: 1.3-mile lollipop
Hiking time: About 45 minutes
Difficulty: Easy
Trail surface: Dirt and crushed gravel
Best season: Spring through fall
Other trail users: Hikers only
Canine compatibility: Dogs not permitted

Fees and permits: None
Schedule: Open daily sunrise to sunset
Map: USGS Fort Collins
Trail contact: Colorado State University Environmental Learning Center, (970) 491-1661, www .csuelc.org

Finding the trailhead: From North College Avenue (US 287) and East Drake Road, go east on Drake 2.7 miles to Environmental Drive. Take a left and go 0.2 mile to a sign for the Environmental Learning Center. Take a left here, cross the railroad tracks, and travel a dirt road 0.2 mile to the parking lot on the right. GPS: N40 33.23' / W105 01.10'

The Hike

Among the trails in town, the CSU Environmental Learning Center Trails offer up a nice variety of features, including a suspension footbridge, deciduous trees, a riverside portion of trail, and the opportunity for a quick side trip to a raptor rehabilitation center, which was closed at least temporarily due to avian flu in 2015.

From the parking lot, begin by hopping on the paved Poudre River Trail for about 50 feet—or better yet, ride to the trailhead and lock up (bikes aren't allowed on CSU ELC trails). The footpath parts from the paved trail, takes you across a suspension footbridge (this is not the Poudre River), and drops you off at the beginning of this loop. Here is where you will find a trailhead kiosk and a trail map.

Walking the loop in a counterclockwise direction, take a right. There is a lot of edge habitat here, where cottonwood trees meet grasslands meet water. Look for birds, including hawks, jays, and woodpeckers. As you approach the Poudre River, see a marked spur trail heading downstream. You can follow this a few hundred feet to a sandy beach-like area.

Continuing upstream, get some views of the wild and scenic Poudre River—the best view is from the official viewing deck at mile 1.1, where you will see a rocky bend, another sandy area, cottonwoods, and likely some wildlife. Finish the loop and cross the suspension bridge again to return to the trailhead.

Miles and Directions

0.0 Start at the northwest side of the parking lot on a paved trail, which is a spur of the Poudre River Trail. In about 50 feet, a gravel trail forks off to the right in a break in the (wooden) fence. Take this trail, and in about 150 feet, cross a suspension footbridge and arrive at the beginning of the trail loop. Take a right to begin the loop.

0.2 Come to a fork. Take a right for the Wilcox Trail (left is the Alden Trail, marked with a sign).

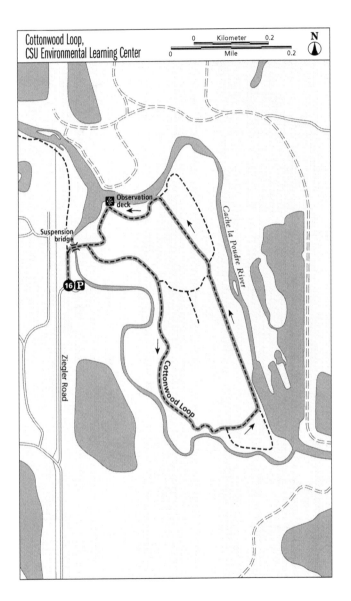

Cottonwood Loop,
CSU Environmental Learning Center

0   Kilometer   0.2
0   Mile   0.2

N

Observation deck

Suspension bridge

Cache la Poudre River

16 P

Ziegler Road

Cottonwood Loop

0.6 Arrive at a junction marked with a "spur" and "main trail" sign. Take a left to continue the loop.

1.0 Approach what appears to be a T intersection close to the river. The trail goes left.

1.1 Come to an overlook deck along the river's edge. After checking out the view, turn back and continue straight.

1.2 Return to the spot where you began the loop. Cross the suspension bridge and return the way you came.

1.3 Arrive back at the parking lot trailhead.

17 Foothills to Reservoir Loop Trail, Pineridge Natural Area

The trailhead sign for the Foothills and Reservoir Loop Trails could read "Welcome to Prairie Dog Town." The southern half of this loop, which rings the 40-acre Dixon Reservoir, takes you through a prairie dog town. To the southwest you will see, as the name suggests, a pine-covered ridge.

Distance: 2.0-mile loop
Hiking time: About 1 hour
Difficulty: Easy
Trail surface: Dirt road and trail
Best season: Summer through winter
Other trail users: Mountain bikes, equestrians
Canine compatibility: Leashed dogs permitted
Fees and permits: None
Schedule: Open daily 5 a.m. to 11 p.m.

Maps: USGS Horsetooth Reservoir; City of Fort Collins Natural Areas map
Trail contact: City of Fort Collins Natural Areas, (970) 416-2815, fcgov.com/naturalareas/finder/pineridge
Special considerations: There is no water at the trailhead so bring your own. Check for trail closures due to muddy conditions at www.fcgov.com/naturalareas/status.php or #FCTrails on Twitter.

Finding the trailhead: From US 287 (South College Road) and Drake Road, take West Drake Road 2.9 miles to where it ends at South Overland Trail. Turn right (north) and go 0.2 mile to CR 42C. Turn left (west) and travel 0.8 mile to the entrance on the left. Drive to the second parking area, which has a pit toilet and two covered picnic tables. GPS: W40 33.06' / W105 08.35'

The Hike

Easy is one of the best words to describe this trail. Easy access. Easy hiking. Easy wildlife viewing. All of these factors contribute to the popularity of the Pineridge Natural Area, which was part of the first purchase the city made for these natural areas, back in 1976.

Expect to share the wide trail with anglers, equestrians, and mountain bikers. The reservoir is a reliable place to view bird life, especially Canada geese and ducks. Ospreys and bald eagles have also been sighted here. There are several edge zones, from where the land meets the water to where the grasslands meet the cottonwoods, willows, and aspen that edge the lake to the beginning of a ponderosa pine forest on the ridge. The trails can get quite muddy in the spring.

Descend from the parking lot down toward the water and hike north to the dam. Cross the dam and walk the length of the east side of the reservoir to the south. You will hear the squeaks and see the telltale mounded landscape created by the prairie dogs that have taken up residence here. The prairie dogs are adorable but not uncontroversial. The Fort Collins Natural Areas management plan calls for balancing a healthy prairie dog population with a healthy ecosystem. In several natural areas the prairie dogs have caused significant soil erosion.

The plague has drastically reduced the size of this prairie dog town at different times, and then the dogs have built up their population again. In addition to removing some prairie dogs in city natural areas, in 2014 endangered black-footed ferrets were let loose at Soapstone Prairie Natural Area to prey on the prairie dogs.

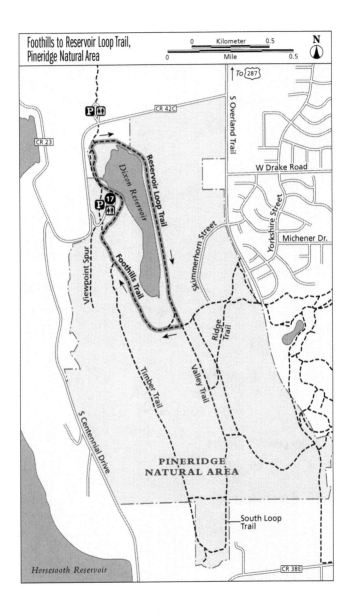

Foothills to Reservoir Loop Trail,
Pineridge Natural Area

Kilometer

Mile

N

To 287

CR 42C

CR 23

P

Dixon Reservoir

Reservoir Loop Trail

P 17

S Overland Trail

W Drake Road

Yorkshire Street

Michener Dr.

Skimmerhorn Street

Viewpoint Spur

Foothills Trail

Ridge Trail

Valley Trail

Timber Trail

S Centennial Drive

PINERIDGE
NATURAL AREA

South Loop
Trail

CR 38E

Horsetooth Reservoir

Miles and Directions

0.0 Start at the trailhead just left (west) of the pit toilet. Walk through a gate and descend the hill. In about 400 feet, come to a junction where the Foothills Trail is signed. Go straight.

0.3 Come to a T intersection. The Foothills Trail continues to the left. Take a right and begin the Reservoir Loop Trail. Cross the dam and then walk the length of the reservoir.

1.1 Arrive at a four-way junction with shortcut trails. Take the second right to walk around the southern end of the reservoir.

1.7 Come to a junction with the marked Timber Trail to the left. Continue straight (north).

1.8 Pass an access trail on the left for the first parking area. Continue straight.

2.0 Look to your left to see a long series of steps. Take the steps up to the parking area where you began.

18 Coyote Ridge Trail, Coyote Ridge Natural Area

Tackle this trail at sunrise or sunset (or moonrise or moonset) to avoid the scorching sun of midday and to increase your chances of seeing wildlife like coyotes and mountain lions.

Distance: 4.2 miles out and back
Hiking time: About 2 hours
Difficulty: Easy
Trail surface: Dirt road and rocky trail
Best season: Any season, but avoid midday
Other trail users: Mountain bikers, equestrians
Canine compatibility: Dogs not permitted
Fees and permits: None
Schedule: 5 a.m. to 11 p.m. daily

Maps: USGS Masonville; Fort Collins Natural Areas map
Trail contact: City of Fort Collins Natural Areas, (970) 416-2815, fcgov.com/naturalareas/finder/coyote
Special considerations: Do not leave valuables in your car, as break-ins have been reported. The parking lot fills early on weekends and parking regulations are strictly enforced—do not park along the road.

Finding the trailhead: From South College Avenue (US 287) in north Loveland, take Trilby Road west 1.9 miles to South Taft Hill Road. Take a left (south) on Taft Hill and go 0.9 mile to the trailhead parking on the right (west) side of the road, marked as Spring Mesa Road. GPS: N40 28.51' / W105 06.58'

The Hike

Coyote Ridge is decidedly not a walk in the woods, so plan accordingly and enjoy the open spaces, wildlife, and a rewarding view after you ascend the ridge. Begin by walking due west in the high plains toward the foothills. This is a grassland area dotted with mullein and yucca. You will definitely see prairie dogs and birds, and you'll have a good chance of eyeing rattlesnakes, coyotes, or mule deer.

In a mile reach a cabin (and a pit toilet). The Hidden Clues Trail is a 0.2-mile interpretive trail behind the cabin. The Coyote Ridge Trail is about to start its ascent to the top of the ridge. Pass behind and then eventually hike above a hogback ridge. The trail is somewhat steep, but switchbacks (and rests) make it a manageable walk to the top of the ridge.

At the top of the ridge, you will be rewarded with views of a dry valley to the west, long hogback ridges running north and south, and high mountain peaks on the western horizon. Sit at a bench by a hitching post and explore some trees and rocks before you descend the ridge.

This hike is wide and open—especially the first mile—so you can comfortably start before dawn or finish after dark in order to take advantage of good weather conditions and to have a better chance at viewing wildlife.

Miles and Directions

0.0 Pick up the trailhead at the west end of the parking lot. It is paved for about 100 feet and leads to the trailhead kiosk. Walk past that and join a dirt road. Continue walking west on the dirt road.

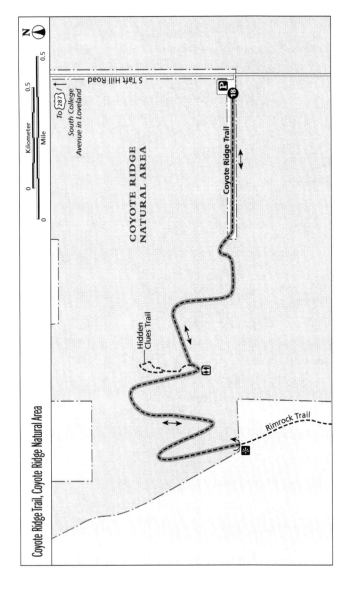

Coyote Ridge Trail, Coyote Ridge Natural Area

N

Kilometer
0   0.5

Mile
0   0.5

To 287
South College
Avenue in Loveland

S Taft Hill Road

COYOTE RIDGE
NATURAL AREA

Hidden
Clues Trail

Coyote Ridge Trail

Coyote Ridge Trail

Rimrock Trail

18

P

1.0 Arrive at a cabin and a pit toilet. The main trail continues to the left of the pit toilet and then switches back right. (***Option:*** You can walk to the cabin and then past it to join the main trail, or you can explore the 0.2-mile Hidden Clues Trail behind the cabin.)

1.6 Come to a side trail to the left next to an interpretive sign titled "Rocky Shrublands." The main trail switches back right.

2.1 Gain the top of the ridge, where you will find some trees, a stone bench, and views to the west. After taking a break, return the way you came.

4.2 Arrive back at the trailhead.

19 Cattail Flats Trail, Fossil Creek Reservoir Natural Area

This is the ultimate birding hike. Bald eagles are common here in the winter, avocets are common in the summer, and you can hear the distinctive and melodious song of the western meadowlark year-round.

Distance: 1.7-mile lollipop
Hiking time: About 1 hour
Difficulty: Easy
Trail surface: Gravel and dirt path with a paved section
Best season: Early spring
Other trail users: Hikers only
Canine compatibility: Dogs not permitted
Fees and permits: None
Schedule: Open year-round, dawn to dusk

Maps: USGS Loveland; Fort Collins Natural Areas map
Trail contact: City of Fort Collins Natural Areas, (970) 416-2815, fcgov.com/naturalareas
Special consideration: The Cattail Flats Trail is closed Dec-Feb, but other trails are open and Eagle Watch programs occur during this time period.

Finding the trailhead: From US 287 and Carpenter Road on the south side of Fort Collins, travel east on Carpenter Road 3.8 miles to the Fossil Creek Reservoir entrance on the left (north) side of the road. Park in the lot by the ranger station. GPS: N40 29.02' / W105 00.58'

The Hike

Fossil Creek Reservoir is a National Audubon Society–designated Important Bird Area. The wide, flat Cattail Flats Trail frees you from looking at your feet so you can look skyward for some of the hundreds of bird species that are found here, either seasonally or year-round. The rock stars of this place are the bald eagles that call Fossil Creek Reservoir home over the winter. There are Eagle Watch programs December through February, but the Cattail Flats Trail is closed then. You will still have a good chance to see eagles from the other trails.

Begin hiking on a paved trail that starts between the ranger station and the amphitheater. You can pick up a brochure here and also a bird checklist. Birds that are easy to sight include great blue herons, mergansers (a species of duck), flickers, swallows, goldfinches, and magpies.

As you begin your walk, look to the right for a chalkboard where hikers can record recent sightings. This will give you a good idea of what to look—and listen—for on your hike. The paved portion of your walk is called the Heron Loop Trail (that's right, for the great blue and other herons that are found here). But even the unpaved Cattail Flats Trail is wheelchair accessible, if not precisely wheelchair friendly.

As you head east on the Cattail Flats Trail, you will begin in an open grassland. Listen for the call of the western meadowlark, elsewhere often found perching on fence posts, but here mostly hanging out in the grass. However, there are posts scattered about for these birds to perch on. Look for the bright-yellow breast with a black V shape. As the loop portion of the trail curves north toward the water, look for water-loving birds on the reservoir, along the shore, and in the cottonwoods above.

Take a few minutes to stop at the bird blind and see a convenient list of common birds, with drawings, that you might view from the blind. Complete the loop and then return in the grassland again to the trailhead.

Cattail Flats Trail, Fossil Creek Reservoir Natural Area

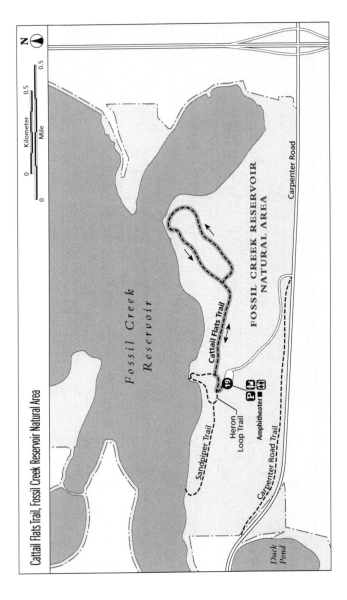

Be sure to leave Fido at home, as Fossil Creek Reservoir is an open space designed to provide habitat for wildlife. Dogs are not permitted because they disturb wildlife, even if left in the car, which is also not allowed.

Miles and Directions

0.0 Start at the paved walkway between the ranger station and amphitheater. Walk north toward the water. In about 150 feet, come to a T intersection and take a right onto the paved Heron Loop Trail. In another 300 feet arrive at the junction with the dirt-and-gravel Cattail Flats Trail. Take a right.

0.4 Arrive at the junction where the loop begins. Take a right to walk in a counterclockwise direction.

0.9 Come to a bird blind on the north side of the trail. After checking it out, continue straight on the trail.

1.2 Return to the junction where you began the loop. Continue straight.

1.6 Return to the junction with the paved Heron Loop Trail. Take a left. In 300 feet take a left and walk back to the trailhead.

1.7 Arrive back at the trailhead.

20 Devil's Backbone Trail Wild Loop, Devil's Backbone Open Space

Ever noticed how many natural features are named with the devil in mind? Devil's Tower. Devil's Lake. Devil's Rock Pile. And here, Devil's Backbone. But the only thing devilish about this trail is the summer midday temperatures in this open space with few specks of shade. It would better be described as heavenly in terms of access, infrastructure, and vistas.

Distance: 2.0-mile lollipop
Hiking time: About 1 hour
Difficulty: Easy
Trail surface: Rocky dirt trail
Best season: Spring or fall
Other trail users: Mountain bikers, equestrians
Canine compatibility: Leashed dogs permitted
Fees and permits: None
Schedule: Sunrise to sunset daily

Maps: USGS Masonville; Larimer County Natural Resources Department recreation map
Trail contact: Larimer County Natural Resources Department, (970) 679-4570, www.co.larimer .co.us/parks/bbone.cfm
Special consideration: This is a popular trail and the parking lot fills up fast on weekends.

Finding the trailhead: From the junction of US 34 and US 287 in Loveland, travel west on US 34 4 miles to Hidden Valley Drive. Take a right and go 0.2 mile to the entrance. Take a left at the entrance to access the parking lot (straight is a private drive). GPS: N40 24.44' / W105 09.10'

The Hike

Fill up with water at a trailhead spigot before starting on this loop, which should take an hour or less to walk. First pass a cottonwood-shaded picnic area and negotiate some steps and footbridges before accessing the Wild Loop of the Devil's Backbone Trail.

To your west is the obvious geological centerpiece of this land. The Devil's Backbone, a so-called hogback ridge, juts up as much as 100 feet from the ground and continues for the length of the hike and beyond in a north-south direction. You're in an open grassland with mountain mahogany and rabbitbrush shrubs the dominant species. Spring wildflowers here include sand lily, wallflower, vetch, and blue flax. Look for prickly poppy and larkspur in the summer and dense clusters of aster in the fall.

Notice the hairy coyote scat along the trail, and listen for their howls. You might also see mule deer and elk. Skyward, you have a good chance of viewing raptors such as red-tailed hawks and kestrels. Ravens nest here.

At the 0.75-mile mark, there is a spur trail to an overlook. To the west you can see Longs Peak and the other Front Range mountains in Rocky Mountain National Park and beyond. On a clear day, look to the southern horizon along the Front Range and see Pikes Peak. Continue north on the trail and take the Keyhole spur trail. The Keyhole is a centerpiece of the Devil's Backbone, an approximately 20-foot-high opening in the rock that affords you similar views of the previous overlook, but this time framed nicely by the rock itself.

As you return southward along the loop, remember to look west again to view the Keyhole from a distance.

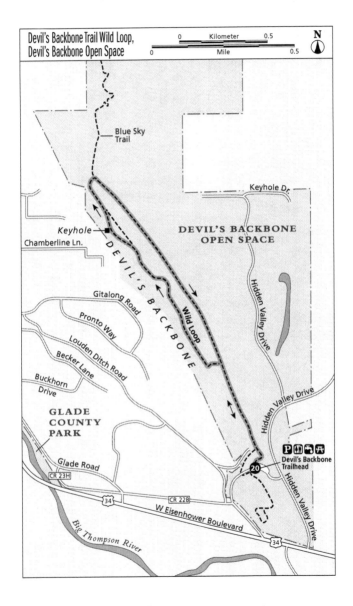

Devil's Backbone Trail Wild Loop,
Devil's Backbone Open Space

Kilometer
0   0.5
Mile
0   0.5

N

Blue Sky
Trail

Keyhole Dr.

Keyhole

Chamberline Ln.

DEVIL'S BACKBONE
OPEN SPACE

Gitalong Road

Pronto Way

Louden Ditch Road

Becker Lane

Buckhorn
Drive

D E V I L ' S   B A C K B O N E

Wild Loop

Hidden Valley Drive

Hidden Valley Drive

GLADE
COUNTY
PARK

Glade Road

CR 23H

34

CR 22B

W Eisenhower Boulevard

34

Big Thompson River

Devil's Backbone
Trailhead

20

Hidden Valley Drive

Miles and Directions

0.0   Start at the trailhead kiosk, located near the pit toilets. Begin on the trail and go about 400 feet, passing a picnic area, ascending steps, and then crossing two footbridges.

0.4   Come to a fork. Take the left fork to begin the Wild Loop.

0.8   Come to a junction. Take a left and walk about 50 feet to an overlook of Longs Peak and other Front Range peaks. Return to the junction and take a left, continuing north.

1.0   Come to a junction with the Keyhole spur. Take a left and ascend the ridge toward the Keyhole (GPS: N40 25.16' / W105 09.37').

1.2   Come to a junction where you return to the Loop Trail. Continue straight, heading north.

1.3   Arrive at a three-way junction. Turn right and head south to start heading back to the trailhead.

1.6   Return to the junction where you began the Wild Loop. Continue straight (south) the way you came from the trailhead.

2.0   Arrive back at the trailhead.

21 Valley Loop Trail, Bobcat Ridge Natural Area

This is an appropriately named trail—walk a nearly 4-mile loop in a wide-open valley with views of red rock outcroppings, mountains, and sky. This natural area is home to most of the Front Range's most exciting wildlife, including mountain lions, bears, and its namesake bobcats.

Distance: 3.9-mile loop
Hiking time: About 2 hours
Difficulty: Easy
Trail surface: Crushed gravel and rocky trail
Best season: Year-round
Other trail users: Equestrians and mountain bikers
Canine compatibility: Dogs not permitted

Fees and permits: None
Schedule: Open daily dawn to dusk
Maps: USGS Masonville; Fort Collins Natural Areas map
Trail contacts: City of Fort Collins Natural Areas, (970) 416-2815, fcgov.com/naturalareas/finder/bobcat

Finding the trailhead: From US 287 and Harmony Road in Fort Collins, take West Harmony Road (W CR 38E) 9.7 miles to CR 27 (Buckhorn Road) and take a left (south). Go 0.6 mile to CR 32C. Take a right (west) and travel 0.5 mile to the preserve parking lot on the left. GPS: N40 28.46' / W105 13.33'

The Hike

As soon as you pull into the driveway of Bobcat Ridge Natural Area, you get a sense of its recent history as a farmstead. Many of the buildings related to its farming and ranching history still exist, and the oldest cabin dates back to the nineteenth century. It is undoubtedly more fun to hike or ride this land than to farm it.

Your fellow trail users include equestrians and mountain bikers, but no dogs because they disturb the abundant wildlife that calls this place home—from elk and bears to skunks and, of course, bobcats. If you don't see any of the charismatic wildlife on your hike, check out the Bobcat Ridge Wildlife Camera Project at www.fcgov.com/naturalareas/wildlife-camera.php to view some wildlife images recorded by motion-activated cameras.

The trail begins in an open grass-and-shrub land that is rich with rabbitbrush and yucca, and the first mile and a half is graded and maintained to be wheelchair accessible. Look for blue flax blooming in the spring and asters in the fall.

Pick up a bird checklist at the trailhead kiosk and see how many you can identify. Look for raptors, plus wild turkeys, hummingbirds, and sparrows in the open valley. The wide-open scenery includes red rock ridges and distant peaks. As the loop continues, the middle third of the trail takes you up a ridge on a narrow, rocky trail, into some ponderosa pine trees and above the valley floor. Side trails take you to an old cabin and what are thought to be Native American tipi rings, once used in the winter when it was too frozen to place tipi poles directly into the ground.

Miles and Directions

0.0 Start at the far end of the parking lot. Begin on a paved (wheelchair-accessible) path. Pass a kiosk in about 300 feet.

0.1 Approach a T intersection, marked with a trail sign. Take a right and begin the Valley Loop Trail.

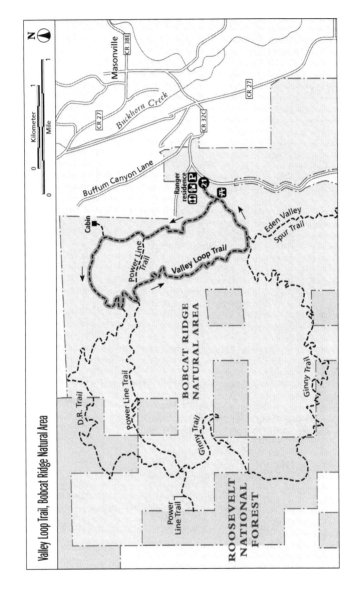

Valley Loop Trail, Bobcat Ridge Natural Area

0.9 Come to a four-way junction with the Power Line Trail. Continue straight.

1.2 Reach another four-way junction. Take a left to continue on the Valley Loop Trail. (Straight is a spur to a historic cabin.) In about 150 feet you'll pass another spur trail to the cabin. Keep straight.

2.0 Come to a fork, which is a junction with the D.R. Trail. Take the left fork.

2.2 Arrive at a four-way junction with the Power Line Trail again. Go straight.

2.4 Reach a junction with the Tipi Loop Trail. Trend right.

3.5 Come to a junction with the Ginny Trail on the right. Continue straight. In a few hundred feet, come to a junction with the Eden Valley Spur Trail. Continue straight.

3.8 Return to the junction where you began the Valley Loop. Take a right and walk back to the trailhead.

3.9 Arrive back at the trailhead.

22 Foothills Nature Trail, Roosevelt National Forest

The enjoyment of this trail begins before you get out of the car—driving through Big Thompson Canyon is a sight to behold. Just a dozen miles from Loveland, you'll be hiking in the forest the entire length of the trail. End with an overlook from a Civilian Conservation Corps–era stone shelter.

Distance: 2.0 miles out and back

Hiking time: 1 hour

Difficulty: Easy

Trail surface: Dirt road grade and rocky dirt trail

Best season: Spring through fall

Other trail users: Hikers only

Canine compatibility: Leashed dogs permitted

Fees and permits: None

Schedule: US Forest Service lands are open 24/7, 365 days a year, but no overnight camping is allowed near the trailhead or along the Foothills Nature Trail

Maps: USGS Drake; Trails Illustrated map 101 (Cache La Poudre/Big Thompson); City of Loveland Foothills Nature Trail brochure

Trail contacts: City of Loveland Parks and Recreation Department, (970) 962-2727, parks@cityofloveland.org. Roosevelt National Forest Canyon Lakes Ranger District, (970) 295-6700, www.fs.usda.gov/main/arp

Special consideration: Rifle-hunting season generally falls in Oct–Nov, so you may want to wear blaze orange or avoid the trails during that time.

Other: Go to the City of Loveland website and download or print the *Foothills Nature Trail* interpretive brochure (www.cityofloveland.org/modules/showdocument.aspx?documentid=8023); it may not be stocked at the trailhead.

Finding the trailhead: From the junction of US 34 and US 287 in Loveland, go west on US 34 for 12.7 miles to the trailhead on the left (south) side of the canyon. GPS: N40 25.13' / W105 17.7'

The Hike

There is perhaps no prettier easy day hike within such a close striking distance to Loveland. Driving the serpentine road to the trailhead through the lower Big Thompson Canyon is eye candy, with steep rock walls jutting above and the Big Thompson River rushing below.

The trail begins jointly with the Round Mountain Recreation Trail and ascends through a ponderosa pine forest on a pipeline access road most of the way. Begin by walking uphill past a gate and keep walking uphill for a mile. After just 0.1 mile, come to an opening in the forest where the Summit Trail (Round Mountain National Recreation Trail) splits from the Foothills Nature Trail. Take a moment to walk toward the canyon overlook, where you will get your best view of the hike. You'll see the road and river below, forested slopes on the other side of the canyon, and lower-elevation peaks in the distance.

If you download or print a brochure from the City of Loveland website, you can take a self-guided nature walk by stopping at the numbered posts. Even without a brochure, you'll notice a couple of obvious trailside features. One is a pipe carrying water from a dam upslope to a hydroelectric plant downslope. This is part of the Colorado–Big Thompson Project, which diverts water from the west side of the Continental Divide to the eastern side of Colorado. The other is evidence of a recent fire, made visible by charred tree trunks.

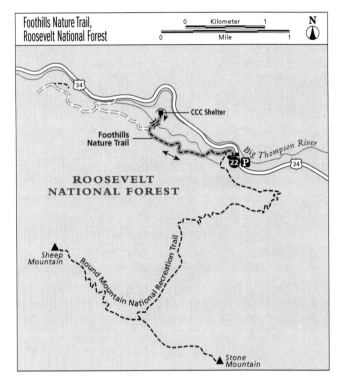

0   Kilometer   1

0   Mile   1

N

CCC Shelter

Foothills
Nature Trail

Big Thompson River

22 P

34

**ROOSEVELT
NATIONAL FOREST**

Sheep
Mountain

Round Mountain National Recreation Trail

Stone
Mountain

The trail ends at a 1930s-era Civilian Conservation Corps (CCC) stone shelter. This Depression-era public works program was part of President Franklin D. Roosevelt's New Deal, and its goal was to put young men to work while conserving the nation's natural resources. You can see this stone-and-beam style of shelter in CCC projects all around the country. Bring lunch since you've got such a good spot to eat it. There is an informal trail that goes past the shelter another 60 feet or so with a better view.

Miles and Directions

0.0   Start at the gate past the pit toilet. Walk around the gate and start ascending on the wide, smooth, road-grade trail.

0.1   Come to a flat, open space where the Summit Trail and Nature Trail split, marked with a sign. Continue straight on the Nature Trail.

0.9   Come to a fork marked with a sign pointing you to the right, to the overlook.

1.0   End at the shelter house. Return the way you came.

2.0   Arrive back at the trailhead.

23 Crosier Mountain Trail, Roosevelt National Forest

There are several lengthy trails to the summit of Crosier Mountain, but this shorter option takes you through a ponderosa pine forest, past an old mine opening, to several vistas, and to a mountain meadow that is a good turnaround point.

Distance: 3.0 miles out and back

Hiking time: About 1.5 hours

Difficulty: Easy

Trail surface: Dirt trail

Best season: Late spring to summer

Other trail users: Mountain bikers, equestrians

Canine compatibility: Controlled dogs permitted

Fees and permits: None

Schedule: US Forest Service lands are open 24/7, 365 days a year

Maps: USGS Glen Haven and Drake; Trails Illustrated map 101 (Cache La Poudre/Big Thompson)

Trail contact: Roosevelt National Forest Canyon Lakes Ranger District, (970) 295-6700, www.fs.usda.gov/main/arp

Special considerations: Rifle-hunting season generally falls in Oct–Nov, so you may want to wear blaze orange or avoid the trails during that time.

Finding the trailhead: From the junction of US 287 and US 34 in Loveland, head west on US 34 16.3 miles to Drake, where the road forks. Take a right onto CR 43 and drive 2.1 miles to the unsigned trailhead parking on the left. It's a dirt lot with room for about six cars. GPS: N40 26.34' / W105 22.41'

The Hike

It may be simply a function of the fact that the trailhead parking can only accommodate about a half dozen vehicles, but the Crosier Mountain Trail (#931) is a great one for solitude—not to mention vistas, wildlife, and wildflowers.

Begin by walking through a gate—be sure to close and secure it behind you. Walk on a gently ascending trail in a meadow where, among the mountain mahogany and rabbit-brush, you'll see locoweed blooming in spring. *Loco* is Spanish for crazy, and when livestock eat this flowering plant, they exhibit the effects of the neurological damage its toxicity causes. Needless to say, keep your pets from eating locoweed. Continue into the forest, which is dominated by ponderosa pine but also contains Douglas fir, juniper, and a few aspen.

At around the 0.8-mile mark, you'll see an old mine opening on the right side of the trail. If you peer in, you'll see an old mine shaft with some roof supports. Little seems to be known about mining operations around here, but look on the Trails Illustrated topo map and you'll see Sullivan Park written south of the Crosier Mountain Trail. Sullivan Park was apparently an old mining operation, and there are still open mining pits around. Because of this, stay on the trail and keep your dog under control. It's interesting to take a flashlight to the open mine shaft, but unless you want to be the subject of a newspaper article about a mine collapse killing a hiker, keep it to just looking from the mouth of the entrance.

After the mine shaft, the trail gets steeper. It's worth continuing another tenth of a mile to the top of a ridge with new views to the south of forested mountains and granite outcroppings. You can hear the North Fork of the Big Thompson River below and the calls of Steller's jays

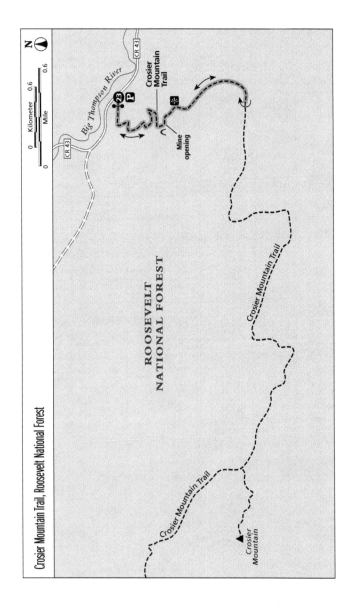

Crosier Mountain Trail, Roosevelt National Forest

and crows on the wing. Black bear sightings along this trail are not uncommon. Continuing up the steepening and then leveling trail, you'll see blackened snags from recent fires. Continue to the meadow, where you'll see grasses and flowers such as pasqueflower and lupine. From here, you can turn around for a 3.0-mile out-and-back, or continue another 3 miles one-way to the peak of 9,250-foot Crosier Mountain.

Miles and Directions

0.0 Start by walking through the gate at the parking area and closing it behind you. Walk west on the trail, paralleling the road about 175 feet to a trailhead sign and map. Continue straight past the sign, and where it looks like the trail forks, stay to the right. There are a number of social trails along this route, but they are blocked off well and it's easy to stay on the trail.

0.8 Walk by (and check out) an old mine entrance on the right side of the trail. From here the trail gets steeper and takes you to a ridgetop in another 0.1 mile.

1.2 Reach a second ridgetop and an informal trail to the left that takes you to a log that's a nice spot to sit and have a break.

1.5 Arrive at a mountain meadow. This is a good lunch and turnaround spot. (*Option:* You can continue as far as the full length of the trail, which is 4.5 miles one-way.)

3.0 Return the way you came to the trailhead.

24 Shoshone to Besant Point Trail Loop, Ramsay-Shockey Open Space

Less than 10 miles up the Big Thompson Canyon, Ramsay-Shockey Open Space provides everything you'd want in a mountain hiking experience: a walk in the woods to mountain vistas plus A-list wildlife. Camping, fishing, and boating are all bonuses.

Distance: 2.5-mile lollipop
Hiking time: About 1.5 hours
Difficulty: Easy
Trail surface: Dirt singletrack and doubletrack
Best season: Fall when elk are bugling
Other trail users: Mountain bikers
Canine compatibility: Leashed dogs permitted

Fees and permits: Day-use fee required
Schedule: Sunrise to sunset daily
Maps: USGS Pinewood Lake; Larimer County Open Spaces map
Trail contact: Larimer County Natural Resources Department, (970) 679-4570, www.co.larimer .co.us/parks/ramsay.cfm

Finding the trailhead: From the junction of US 34 and US 287 in Loveland, take US 34 7.4 miles to S CR 29. Turn left (south) and go 2 miles to Pole Hill Road (CR 18 E). Take a right and go 2 miles to the Larimer County Natural Resources Administrative Building on the left, where you must pick up your day-use permit. Then return to Pole Hill Road and take a left, continuing west for 4.6 miles to the Ramsay-Shockey Trailhead parking on the left. GPS: N40 22.03' / W105 17.06'

The Hike

Pinewood Reservoir is just one of twelve that are part of the Colorado–Big Thompson project, designed to provide a regular water supply to the eastern slope of the Rockies by diverting and storing water from the western slope of the mountains. Fortunately, outdoor recreation was included in the project plans. Begin your hike by walking over the dam that creates the 100-acre reservoir.

On the other side of the dam, walk upslope on the Shoshone Trail, a footpath that takes you through a ponderosa pine forest. Look for bluebells blooming in the spring and larkspur in late spring and summer. You might also see slash piles. These are part of the fire-management plan designed to reduce forest fire hazards.

As the trail reaches the top of the ridge, it turns into a doubletrack. Note the interesting rock outcroppings, which resemble micro versions of the Boulder Flatirons. Before the trail descends from the ridge, you can view both the southern and northern portions of Pinewood Reservoir. After descending to the water's edge, leave the Shoshone Trail—named after the Native Americans who live in the region—and join the Besant Point Trail, named after the prehistoric Native Americans who inhabited this area.

Make sure to take the Fisherman's Cove option where the trail forks and then comes back together. This will take you close to the water and around a rocky cove with a picnic area. End your hike by crossing back over the dam. Look for wildlife that includes everything from the small (Albert's squirrels) to the large (elk) to the winged (blue herons).

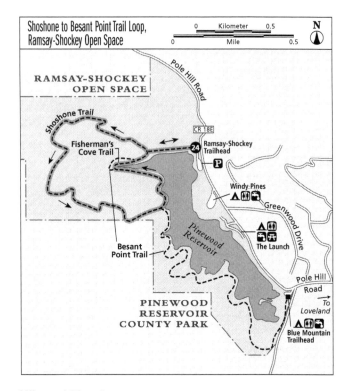

Shoshone to Besant Point Trail Loop, Ramsay-Shockey Open Space

RAMSAY-SHOCKEY OPEN SPACE

Shoshone Trail

Fisherman's Cove Trail

CR 18E

Ramsay-Shockey Trailhead

Windy Pines

Greenwood Drive

The Launch

Besant Point Trail

Pinewood Reservoir

Pole Hill Road

To Loveland

PINEWOOD RESERVOIR COUNTY PARK

Blue Mountain Trailhead

Miles and Directions

0.0 Start at the short section of paved trail and then cross over the dam.

0.3 On the other side of the dam, come to a five-way trail intersection with a pit toilet. Facing the pit toilet, take the trailhead just to the right, marked with a metal "Shoshone" signpost.

1.8 Come to a T intersection with the Besant Point Trail, marked with a sign. Take a left.

2.0 Arrive at a fork. Take the right fork for the Fisherman's Cove Trail, staying near the water.

2.2 Come to a four-way junction with the Besant Point and Fisherman's Cove Trails, also marked with a sign. Go straight, taking the wide path that ascends. In a couple hundred feet, return to the pit toilet where the loop began. Walk back across the dam to the trailhead.

2.5 Arrive back at the trailhead.

Honorable Mention: Young Gulch Trail, Roosevelt National Forest

In 2012 the High Park fire caused extensive damage to the Young Gulch Trail in the Roosevelt National Forest. Volunteers worked tirelessly to rebuild it, opening the route just days before the September 2013 flood. Unfortunately, the flood damaged the newly reopened Young Gulch trail to such an extent that the US Forest Service closed it until it could again be rebuilt. The new trail—expected to open in 2016—will likely take a different track to better position it in the event of future floods.

Once rebuilt, the Young Gulch Trail will again become one of the most popular Poudre Canyon trails. Young Gulch is a scenic and relatively flat area for a hike, featuring an attractive creek and lots of beautiful flora such as ponderosa pine, Douglas fir, and juniper. Pasqueflower peaks in April, pussytoes in May, and barrel cactus and penstemon in summer, all of which will enhance the visual aspect of the hike.

In addition to the foliage, this area also has some notable wildlife. Rattlesnake and brown bear sightings are regularly reported, so take appropriate precautions.

The new trail should follow the gulch and continue for nearly 5 miles toward Stove Prairie Road; however, you will hit private property before arriving at the road. It is important not to trespass and to plan your out-and-back hike accordingly.

Finding the trailhead: From the junction of CO 14 and US 287 north of Fort Collins (Ted's Place), drive west on CO 14 up the Poudre Canyon 12.8 miles. Turn left into the trailhead parking. (These directions are subject to change, depending on how the new trail is tracked.)

Fort Collins-Area Clubs and Trail Groups

Fort Collins Group of the Colorado Mountain Club
Membership organization with hiking, backpacking, and other mountain outings.
(303) 279-3080 (Colorado Mountain Club statewide office)
www.fortcmc.org

Poudre Wilderness Volunteers
Volunteer wilderness rangers assisting the Canyon Lakes Ranger District of the US Forest Service.
PO Box 271921
Fort Collins, CO 80527
http://pwv.org

Meetup
A number of hiking-related meetup groups are based in Fort Collins:
http://hiking.meetup.com/cities/us/co/fort_collins/

About the Author

Mary Reed is a freelance journalist whose work has appeared in *Backpacker*, *Boulder Magazine*, *Boulder Weekly* and many other publications. She is the author of *Hiking West Virginia* and *Hiking Ohio* (also FalconGuides). She lived in Fort Collins when she attended Colorado State University. She now lives in Athens, Ohio, and Boulder, Colorado.

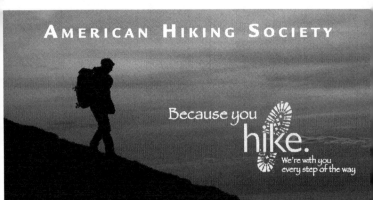

The
Christmas
Blanket

KANDI STEINER

Published by Kandi Steiner
Edited by Elaine York/Allusion Publishing
www.allusionpublishing.com
Cover Photography by Perrywinkle Photography
Cover Design by Kandi Steiner
Formatting by Elaine York/Allusion Publishing
www.allusionpublishing.com

"I am lost without you.
What a hauntingly beautiful thing
to say to a person — that whether
you are off on another wild adventure
or in the familiar quiet comfort of your very own
home, you are all the same, enormously lost,
whenever you are without them."

— *Beau Taplin*

Off the Beaten Path

"*Have a holly, jolly whoamygodshiiiii!*"

I braked as gently as I could, holding onto my wheel for dear life and squinting through the windshield of the rental car I'd picked up from the Burlington airport. Burl Ives continued singing his merry cheer through the car speakers, but I was too busy trying to keep my car on the slick road that was quickly covering with snow to join him.

"Jesus Christ," I breathed when the car was steady again, and I slowed even more, practically to a crawl since I'd already been going just twenty miles per hour. But that was how it went when you were driving in the snow in Vermont, and I

remembered well how awful it could be and how conditions could change at a moment's notice.

Add that to the list of things I did not miss when I moved away.

My knuckles were white where they held the wheel steady, and I cursed under my breath as the sun set even more, the snow falling quicker as the sky got darker. I shouldn't have been surprised to find snow in my path once I pulled off the highway and on the backroads that would lead me to my parents' house in eastern Vermont, but expected or not, I knew the last thirty minutes of my drive would not be fun.

I tried to relax, blowing out a breath and humming along to the next Christmas song that filled my car. The music, coupled with me being back in Vermont for the first time in four years, had me faintly feeling the Christmas spirit, something I hadn't had even a hint of since I was a teenager.

I could already envision the Christmas tree in the corner of my parents' living room, ornaments my sister and I had made throughout childhood hanging from the limbs. I could smell Mom's pumpkin pie, and Grandma's stuffing, and Dad's pineapple brown sugar ham.

My stomach growled as a smile spread on my face. Driving through the snow sucked, but soon, I'd be home again.

There was another pinch in my stomach, one not born of hunger, when I remembered who else would be waiting for me in Wellhaven. Not that he knew I was coming, or would care that I was back, and he *certainly* wouldn't want to see me.

But he'd be there, nonetheless.

And just that fact was enough to twist my guts.

I took a right on the old county road a mile from Lake Wellhaven, the lake our little town was built on, knowing it wouldn't be long now. Just a couple miles, a left, a bumpy old road and a long, worn-out driveway separated me from a hug from my mama.

And the best thing was that she didn't even know I was coming.

Ever since I left Wellhaven four years ago, freshly twenty-four with a dream in my heart and a goodbye kiss on my mama's cheek, she'd been begging me to come back for a holiday. Christmas, Thanksgiving, Easter — hell, she told me President's Day would be just fine, as long as

she could see me. But I'd been on an adventure of my own, one that hadn't made it possible for me to come back home.

Until now.

The last four years had taken me all over the world — South Africa, Europe, Asia, Canada, Mexico. Most recently, I'd been on a work visa in New Zealand for the spring and first part of summer, which was fall and winter here, and I'd made it back to the states just in time to surprise my family for Christmas.

And for the snow to surprise *me*.

The negative temperatures and blistering wind outside my rental car were a drastic change from the beautiful, sunny, sixty-to-seventy degrees I'd left behind. I found myself wondering if I should have just spent the holidays there, hiking through the mountains or working on whatever yacht needed an extra crew member.

But as beautiful and as rich as New Zealand was, it didn't have my family.

And I missed my family dearly.

A thick swallow found my throat as I made the left onto one of the oldest, bumpiest roads in our town, and I slowed the car even more, knowing that one false move on this bad boy

when it was snowing would have me in the ditch. It felt like only yesterday that I'd driven on this same road the opposite way, hightailing my ass out of this town and swearing I wouldn't be back.

I needed adventure.

I needed to explore, to travel, to be free of the crushing reality of the small town I'd grown up in.

I needed to be free of *him*.

I shook my head, and the image of pine-green eyes that seemed to haunt me even still, keeping my focus on the road.

But it didn't matter.

Focusing or not, the best damn driver in the northeast or an out-of-stater driving in the snow for the very first time, nothing could have prevented what happened next.

The front left tire of my car hit a pothole buried under the snow, sending me skidding across the ice. It was getting late, the last of the sun fading, temperatures dropping, and all of that combined with the fresh snow left a slick sheet of ice on that shady part of the road that I just didn't see.

I gripped the wheel as best I could, holding it steady, trying to slow down without braking too

hard, but the car wouldn't comply with my will. I cursed myself for not thinking to get an SUV or at least some snow tires, but I hadn't expected a storm. I was still thinking of what I could've, would've, *should've* done when the wheels started to slide toward the left side of the road. I knew even when I did it that I involuntarily cranked the wheel too much, but it was too late to correct my mistake.

The car whipped around, sliding in reverse off the edge of the road and into the snowy ditch.

I stopped with a quiet *thunk* of metal against snow, or perhaps metal against the mud I knew was *under* that snow. I didn't give myself time to think too much on it, though, before I was gassing it.

"Come on, come on," I prayed under my breath as the wheels spun under me. Snow and mud went flying in my rearview mirror, the front wheels trying to find traction but coming up short. Every time it would move a little, hope would surge in my chest, but just as quickly I'd slide backward.

"Fuck!"

I let off the gas, dropping my head back to the headrest and forcing as much of a calming

breath as I could in that moment. The snow was coming down even harder now, the wind picking up, and I knew I needed to get out of my car and find some traction for these wheels — fast — or I'd be in trouble.

I checked the signal on my phone, knowing before I looked that there'd be no service. There never was on this road, or most of the roads out past the little village on the lake. Wellhaven might as well have been the middle of the ocean when it came to cell service.

Calling my dad wasn't an option, but I knew if I could just find some wood and stick it under the tires, get some traction... I could be on the road and at my parents in twenty.

I shrugged on my coat, put on my gloves, and pulled my thick, knitted beanie over my ears. Then, with one final breath and a silent *you can do this*, I shoved the driver-side door open.

And instantly, my breath was stolen.

It didn't matter how thick my coat or hat or gloves were. It didn't matter that I'd had the heat blasting inside the car. It didn't matter that I'd at least been smart enough to put on my good, warm boots before leaving the airport. No amount of clothing could have prepared me for

that icy wind.

I was already shivering when I rounded the back of the car to assess the damage, and when I saw the snow already piling up around the tires, my stomach sank.

This was not good.

I used the flashlight on the back of my phone, looking at the ditch and the woods behind it. Surely there would be some piece of scrap wood I could use for traction. I headed in that direction, squinting against the fluffy white flakes falling from the sky. One step, and my boot was covered in snow. A second step, and the snow hit my calf.

There was no option but to just go through the ditch, but I knew it wasn't safe to be outside in this weather for too long.

I steeled a breath, preparing myself to be waist deep in the snow, but before I could take another step, a loud, deep voice called from behind me.

"Hey! You alright?!"

The voice was muffled by the wind, and I turned, hopeful, knowing whoever it was could help me. This was the beauty of Small Town America that I missed — there was always someone around to extend a neighborly hand.

The fear that had been niggling at my belly subsided, and I found my first breath since the car slid off the road.

I waved my hands in the air. "I need help! My car's stuck!"

My savior was just a shadow in the dusk as he approached me, a big bundle of fabric behind the bright light of his flashlight. I climbed my way back to the side of the road, turning off my own flashlight that wasn't doing much anyway. There was no other car or truck around, so I assumed the man had joined me from the end of the dirt driveway he was walking away from now.

Oh, thank God, I thought. *Just some wood and a quick push and I'll be on my way. Or maybe this guy's got a big truck and a tow hitch and he can just pull me out.*

I was already smiling when the man reached me, and I shook my head, thumbing over my shoulder to the car. "Guess these rental cars aren't made for driving on these roads in the snow, huh?" I joked.

But when the flashlight lowered and my eyes adjusted, all semblance of humor left me in a whoosh.

Because the man wasn't my savior at all.

He was my ex-husband.

All But Forgotten

This can't be happening.

Even as I prayed the words in my head, I knew it was. I knew that my ever-reliable bad luck had delivered my ex to me within ten minutes of being back in the town limits. I knew it was none other than River Jensen standing there before me.

I would know that man anywhere.

I'd know the line of his jaw — dusted in stubble because he never could grow a beard, and the curve of his nose — broken in ninth grade at a baseball game, and the shape of his torso — lean and narrow at the waist, broad and proud at the shoulders. I'd know the thick brown hair, even hidden under his hat, though it didn't look as long as I'd remembered. And of course, I'd know those furrowed brows, the deep wrinkle between them, and the earthy green eyes they sheltered, too.

I'd never forget those eyes.

Not as long as I lived.

I was still standing there shocked stupid, trying to convince myself it couldn't possibly be my ex-husband and the number-one reason I left this town who'd come to save me and get my car out of the ditch when the bastard let out a long, heavy sigh of his own.

"You've got to be fucking kidding me."

At that, my senses came back to me like the snap of a rubber band.

I narrowed my eyes with a cross of my arms over my chest. "Well, hello to you, too."

River ignored my remark, gesturing to the mess behind me with his big bear paw of a gloved hand. "What the hell kind of car is that to be driving in a blizzard, Eliza?"

I shivered at the sound of my name in that gruff voice, somehow familiar and yet reminiscent of another life I questioned if I'd even lived at all.

"And what are you doing driving in a blizzard at *all*, period?"

"Excuse me," I said, pressing a hand to my chest. "Don't be rude. I just got here."

"No shit."

I frowned. "I drove here straight from the airport, okay? I thought I'd make it before the sun set. Forgive me if I miscalculated." I shook my head. "I see you haven't changed."

He ignored my dig, still assessing the car behind me. "Did you also forget to check the weather forecast before booking your flight?"

"Of course not," I scoffed, but my cheeks heated from the truth, which was that I hadn't even considered it. "I'm very capable of driving on these roads in a little snowstorm. I grew up here, in case you forgot."

A shadow of something passed over his eyes at those words, but he neglected to answer, shaking his head, instead. "A blizzard isn't a little snowstorm."

As if he'd conjured it, a gust of wind so cold and strong blew through the trees, stinging my face and making my eyes water.

"Come on, let's get inside."

River was already on his way back up the hill to that driveaway I assumed he'd joined me from, and from his recommendation to *get inside*, I knew now that I was right.

But I stood rooted in place.

"No, thank you."

At that, he stopped, turning on the heel of his boot with a cocked brow. "No, thank you?"

"I'm going to get some wood to put under the back tires and be on my way," I said firmly, already heading back toward the woods. "If you'd be so kind as to help me, I'd appreciate it. But if you'd rather be on your way, don't let me stop you."

He chuckled, and the sound sent a wave of fury through me.

"A little wood isn't going to get that car unstuck," he said.

"I've used that trick a dozen times before," I argued back, but somehow I had stopped, facing him again with a popped hip and a *watch me* attitude.

"That may be so, but those wheels are already half buried, and so is any scrap of anything you'd find in those woods. It'll also be wet. And of no use."

I looked over my shoulder at the woods, chewing on his observation and hating that he was probably right.

Another gust of wind whipped through, and I was shivering so hard now I didn't know if I could stand another minute outside. My feet were numb. My hands, too. My eyes stung from the wind, and my nose was threatening to divorce me if I didn't get some warm air on it.

But the alternative was going inside with *him.*

I shook my head. "I'll figure something out."

I started making my way toward the ditch, remembering I'd have to climb through it to get to the woods, and that I'd have to ignore my numb, aching feet in the process. I expected River to leave, but instead he let out another deep and heavy sigh, and then he was trudging past me and ripping the back driver-side door open on my little rental car.

"Hey!" I said when he heaved out my suitcase, lugging the thing over his shoulder like it weighed nothing. "Put that back!"

But he ignored me, his boots leaving fresh prints in the snow as he marched right past me and toward the driveway he'd come out from.

I stood there, gaping, looking at the car and then at him with my suitcase and back again at least a half-dozen times. The snow was falling harder and harder, the wind unbearable, and as much as it was the absolute last thing I wanted to do, I knew I had no choice.

I let out something between a growl and a scream, though not loud enough that he could hear it, and then I stomped back to the car and leaned in long enough to grab my purse. I slammed the door, hit the lock button, and jogged to catch up to the grumpy man carrying the rest of my things.

I'll just get inside, warm up, and call Dad.

No big deal.

"You're insufferable," I said when I finally caught up to him.

"Aren't you glad you left?"

"If only I'd had the good sense to stay gone."

His jaw ticked, but he said nothing, adjusting my bag on his shoulder.

And we walked the rest of the way to the cabin at the end of the drive in silence.

Can You Hear Me Now?

I didn't take the time to marvel at the little A-frame cabin River led us up to — mostly because every part of my body was just about frozen by the time we made it to the front door. Instead, I happily followed him inside when he shoved the door open, every molecule of my being rejoicing at the rush of warm air that greeted us.

And the very next instant, a pair of paws greeted me, too — landing right on the center of my chest and pushing me back against the door River had just closed.

I let out a squeak, squinting against the slobbery tongue assaulting my face. It stung against my cold cheeks, and I would have been annoyed or pissed off if River wouldn't have said the next words he did.

"That's enough, Moose," he said. "Down boy."

River didn't even raise his voice, it was just a low, firm command. But Moose obeyed, just like he always had, and all the shock and displeasure faded in an instant at the sound of his name.

"Moose?" I asked, first to the dog, and then my eyes found River's. "*Our* Moose?"

River's jaw ticked, but he otherwise said nothing, dropping my suitcase to the floor with a *thud*.

Moose was making the strangest squealing noises I'd ever heard, and I knew it took every ounce of willpower that mutt had to keep his ass on the floor as he looked up at me with his tongue lolling out of his mouth. His tail was waving furiously, his mahogany brown fur long and silky just like I remembered, although the fur around his mouth was peppered with gray now, and he had the same scar over his nose from when we'd first found him abandoned and bleeding in the woods.

"Oh my *God*, it really is you!" I dropped to my knees then, opening my arms, and that was the only permission Moose needed to leap onto me once more. I fell backward at the impact, my petite frame no match for the ninety pounds of muscle that dog had on him, but I was laughing all the same as he licked my cheeks, my chin, still making those same squealing noises.

"Traitor," River murmured under his breath, and then he left us at the door, shrugging off his coat and hanging it on the rack by the fireplace.

"I can't believe you still have him," I marveled, rubbing Moose behind the ears. I didn't care that his breath smelled like he'd been eating dead skunks for dinner a week straight — I never thought I'd see this dog again, and now that he was in my arms, I couldn't imagine how I ever left him behind.

"What, did you think I'd just kick him out?" River bit back. And I thought I heard him mumble something under his breath, but couldn't be sure what.

"Of course not," I answered softly, patting Moose's head once more before I stood. I didn't want to say it out loud, but the dog was at least eleven years old now, if not more. We never were sure of his age when we found him. "I guess I'm just surprised to see him, that's all."

19

"Well, today is just full of surprises, isn't it?"

The joy Moose had brought evaporated in an instant, and I frowned, watching as River shook the snow from his boots next before dropping them by the fireplace. He peeled off his hat and gloves, and then it was just him in a pair of dark jeans, a beige, thermal, long-sleeve shirt, and two mismatched socks with holes in the toes.

Nothing had changed, and yet everything had.

River was older than when I'd left, that much was obvious, but now that we were inside and in the warm light of his cabin, I could see it. I could see the lines of his face that weren't there before, the creases of his eyes, the strong line between his brows. I could see the bit of gray dotting his stubble prematurely, something his father had, too, when he was younger. His hair used to be so long it'd curl around the edge of his baseball cap, but now, it was just a fade, cut short and simple. His arms were bigger, his chest, too — the lean frame from the days he'd played ball replaced by a body I barely recognized. It seemed everything about him was more sculpted and manly, such a contrast from the boy who'd stood in my rearview mirror and watched me drive away.

And while I stood there and studied my ex, he didn't so much as give me a second glance before he was headed for the kitchen.

I watched his head disappear inside the old yellow refrigerator long enough to pull out a can of Budweiser, and then he cracked it and drank half in one gulp.

At least some things never change.

Moose was still circling around my feet with a wagging tail as I stripped off my own coat and hung it next to River's on the rack, finally taking in the scene of the small cabin.

It was essentially one large room, the only door one in the back corner that I assumed hid a bathroom. Everything else existed in a sort of chaotic harmony inside the shared space — a tiny kitchen with appliances older than we were, a small folding table cracked at the edges with three mismatched metal chairs around it, a queen-size bed in the corner with navy sheets, two worn pillows, and a simple quilt on top of it. There was a large leather couch that I thought I recognized as the same one his dad used to have in the den, and three shelves of books lining the wall by the fireplace.

It smelled a little like cinnamon, a little like firewood, and a little like whiskey — all wrapped in one.

There seemed to be little projects scattered everywhere else — a half-built something or other in the center of the room, with saw dust and tools littered around it, a half-finished puzzle on the folding table next to a deck of cards splayed out in a half-finished game of solitaire. A book was spread open, face down, the coffee table in front of the couch serving as a bookmark — and it looked halfway finished, too.

So many things started, not a single one completed.

Again, I found myself thinking how some things never change.

I cleared my throat as I unwrapped my scarf, hanging it over my coat. "Well, I would say thank you for helping me, but since you really didn't *help* as much as you forced me against my will into your house..."

"I saved you from hypothermia," he grunted back. "So yeah, you're welcome."

I rolled my eyes.

The sooner I get out of here, the better.

"I would have just called Daddy, if there was any damn cell service on this road," I said, pulling my phone from my back pocket and sliding my thumb over the screen to unlock it. "If you just give me your WiFi password, I can text him and be on my way."

"I don't have one."

I peeled my eyes away from my phone screen where I'd been ready to connect after verifying that, as suspected, I had zero bars of service. "Excuse me?"

"You heard me, Sparrow," he said, leaning a hip against the kitchen counter and taking a sip of his beer. I used to adore that little nickname, but it only made me glare at him now. "No WiFi."

"What do you *mean*, no WiFi?"

"I mean, I don't have it."

I blinked. "I don't understand."

"I don't have it," he said again, slower this time, punctuating each word. "Never have. I don't have a need for it."

"You don't have a need to be connected to the world?" I asked, but then I shook my head, holding up a hand to stop him before he could come up with some smartass remark. "Whatever. Just let me use your house phone, then."

"Don't have one of those, either."

"*What*?" I asked, incredulously and maybe a little too excitedly, since Moose let out a bark and started hopping around my feet again.

I was still staring at River with my mouth open like a trout when he chuckled, tipping his beer toward me. "No Internet. No phone."

I blinked several times. "You have *got* to be kidding me. How the hell do you survive? Don't you work? Don't you need a way to get in touch with people?"

River shrugged. "I work, but I don't need a phone or Internet to do it. And people know where to find me if they need me."

I pinched the bridge of my nose, letting out a sigh I hoped would give me a little patience to survive this interaction. "*Fine*," I gritted through my teeth. "Can you just give me a ride up to Mom and Dad's, please?"

"No can do."

This time, I couldn't help the growl that came from my throat. "You're so maddening! Just take me home so we can both end this nightmare before Christmas."

"Trust me, Eliza, I don't want you here anymore than you want to be here," he said, his voice low and rumbling so much it shook my own chest. His eyes were hard on mine when he crushed the can in his hand and chucked it into the trashcan next to him. "But there's a fucking blizzard going on outside, and whether you planned for that or not doesn't change the fact that it's happening. I can't drive anywhere, and neither can you, and neither can your dad, even if you *could* get in touch with him. *That* is the reality of the situation." He threw his hands up. "Sorry if it doesn't meet your storybook picture you had in mind." Then, he pushed off the counter and dipped back inside the fridge, mumbling the next sentence so low I almost convinced myself I didn't hear it at all. "Just like everything else in your life you left behind here."

The wind howled outside, the wood cabin creaking against the pressure as if to hammer home the point River had just made. And I stood there by the fireplace, obstinate and frustrated, not wanting to take no for an answer.

"So, you're telling me that I'm stuck here?" I deadpanned, gesturing toward him before I let my hand fall against my thigh with a slap. "With you."

"Until the snow lets up and it's safe for either me to drive you, get your car unstuck, or you to walk your happy ass the last dozen miles home?" He cracked open his new beer with a grin that told me he was more pleased than not. "Yep."

The word popped on his lips, and I shook my head, wondering how this could possibly be my life. I hadn't seen River since a week after we signed our divorce papers, on the day I left Wellhaven with a vow to never return.

A vow I stupidly broke, all in the name of being home for the holidays.

I sighed, looking down at Moose who was still wagging his tail furiously and smiling up at me like it was the best day of his life.

That makes one of us, pup.

S·I·S·

A heavy sigh found my chest as I stared at my reflection in the small, dingy mirror of River's bathroom.

As I suspected, the only door in the back corner of his cabin had the bathroom behind it, and it was small, but clean — as clean as an old cabin bathroom could get, anyway.

There was no counter space, save for the small edge around the off-yellow ceramic sink, and it held only River's toothbrush and toothpaste in a little plastic cup. I tried my best to find space for my own toiletries, but ended up setting them on the back of the toilet, since that was the only place they'd fit.

I felt a little more like a functioning human after brushing my teeth and washing my face, changing into a pair of sweatpants and oversized sweater, and pulling on my thickest pair of wool socks. As much as I wanted to pull all my heavy black hair off my neck, I left it there for warmth, seeing as how the fireplace was the only thing warming the entire cabin.

My eyes were just as black as my hair, the brown of the iris so dark you couldn't tell the difference between it and my pupil unless you really stopped to stare. I was uncharacteristically tan for this time of year, thanks to my time in New Zealand, and it made the cream sweater I wore blaze in contrast.

I hadn't even been in Vermont for a full day yet, and already I could feel my lips drying out, so I ran a sheen of lip balm over them and rolled them together, taking in my appearance one last time before I abandoned the bathroom and rejoined my gracious host.

River was still in the kitchen, only this time he was holding his beer in one hand and a spatula in the other, browning hamburger meat on the stove.

That sight hit me like a semi-truck, because with just one blink I could see him ten years younger, doing the exact same thing in the first house we rented together as a couple. His eyes were softer then, younger, not as worn by life.

I'd loved that boy.

I'd loved him since I was twelve years old, before I could even truly understand what love was at all. I'd loved him through all the hell we put each other through, the ups and the downs, the other boys and girls we used mostly to make the other mad or jealous before always finding our way back to each other.

He was the one.

He was the one I'd married two months after high school graduation, the one I'd moved in with two months after graduation without a single hesitation or concern that it wasn't the best decision I could have ever made, and the one I swore I'd spend the rest of my life with — going on adventures, having babies, growing old.

It seemed like another lifetime.

The man who stood before me now was nothing I recognized.

Nothing more than a stranger.

I cleared my throat once I'd shoved my airport clothes in my suitcase, and I held my hands in front of the fireplace, trying to get warm again. Moose had settled into a curled-up ball by the fireplace, too, and his tail wagged gently when I bent down to scratch behind one ear.

"Whatcha making?" I finally asked River after enough awkward silence to last me a year.

"Dinner."

"Obviously," I said as he drained the meat, setting it aside. He put the skillet back on the stove then and added a heap of butter, and I salivated a little as it sizzled to life. "But *what*?"

"Shit on a shingle."

I let out a low, sarcastic laugh through my nose. "S.O.S. How fitting." Then, my nose wrinkled of its own accord. "I can't believe you still eat that stuff."

River shrugged, adding flour to the skillet. "What, you too good for it now?"

"I didn't say that."

"You might as well have." He stirred the ingredients together with more force than necessary. "I didn't expect company, alright? This is what's for dinner. You can have some or not. Up to you."

River poured milk into the mixture on the stove without another word or glance in my direction, and I sighed, looking up to the ceiling like God could help me.

"Look, if we're going to be stuck together, we might as well try to get along," I said, joining him in the kitchen. I grabbed the loaf of bread off the top of the fridge and pulled out six slices — four for him, two for me — and popped the first two in the old toaster on the counter.

River eyed me, but then his brows furrowed once more, and he kept his focus on the gravy.

"You and me, get along?" He shook his head. "When has that ever been the case?"

"So maybe we try something new." I leaned a hip against the counter, crossing my arms and watching him salt and pepper the gravy. "God, this stuff looks so nasty," I said, but couldn't help the smile that spread on my lips next. "But I'd be lying if I said my stomach isn't growling at the smell of it."

Something close to a grunt was the only response I got.

"I remember the first time your dad made this for me," I said after a moment, trying again for civility. "I think we were fourteen? It was sophomore year, after homecoming. We were drunk, and he was so mad at us." I chuckled, remembering the way River's dad had cursed us out the entire way home after picking us up.

"But he also couldn't stop laughing at us. And then he made us this.... this *goop*," I said, waving my hand over the gravy. "*To soak up the booze*," I mimicked in my deepest voice. "Remember that? And he was telling us how it was a staple meal in the military back in the day, and how *his* dad had made it for him. And—"

"I don't really want to go down memory fucking lane, okay?" River slung the ground beef into the gravy mixture he'd made, stirring it a few times before he abandoned it altogether. "Serve yourself."

He walked away without another word, giving me his back as he retreated into the bathroom.

And I just stood there, shocked silent, wondering what I'd said wrong.

Wondering if it was going to be like this until the snow decided to let me out of this cabin jail cell.

The Things We Keep

Unsurprisingly, we ate dinner in silence — me practically done with my plate by the time River rejoined me to make his, smelling faintly of cigarette smoke. I hated that he still had that habit, and found the words to tell him so on the tip of my tongue, but I somehow managed to keep them at bay.

If I was going to be stuck with him for God knew how long, I didn't want to nag him.

I was tired of nagging him.

It was one of the many reasons I'd put him out of his misery and delivered him a divorce.

It seemed so long ago, the conversations that turned into fights that turned into us staring at each other at a complete impasse, knowing this was where we would end. I wanted to get out of this town, see the world, travel, explore. I wanted him to go with me.

He wanted to stay.

It was as simple and as complicated as that.

No matter how I tried to convince him that we could travel and then come back, that we could go see the world and *still* come see our family here at home, he wouldn't budge. He loved the small-town life, where I only longed for more.

And we were so young and so stupidly in love that we didn't think to talk about what we really wanted before we got married.

More than that, what I wanted *changed.*

When I was eighteen, an engagement ring on my finger and a field of butterflies in my heart, being married to River and living here in Wellhaven *was* what I wanted. I wanted the house and the yard and the dog and the kids — just like my parents had, and his parents, too.

But something in me shifted around age twenty-three.

Suddenly, more and more of our friends were coming home from college, or from traveling the world. I would look online and see photos of our friends in exotic countries, eating amazing food, seeing amazing sights. I listened to them talk about their time at college, the classes they took, the parties they went to, the sporting events and bars and clubs and travels abroad.

And I realized it then — there was only so much living you could do in a small town.

I can't explain the thirst that was born in me then. I didn't just want to get out, I *had* to get out — just as much as I had to inhale my next breath in order to keep surviving. My dreams were overhauled, and no longer did I envision the house and the kids — at least, not as soon. Instead, I saw River and myself drinking wine in Italy, snorkeling off the coast of Australia, taking a dip in the hot springs in Iceland, hell, even hiking the mountains in Oregon.

I didn't even consider it, the possibility that River wouldn't want those same things.

But when I brought it all up to him, you would have thought I'd told him I cheated on him with his best friend.

He wanted nothing to do with it. He wouldn't entertain the possibility of leaving. He wouldn't even consider taking a long *vacation* when I proposed that as a compromise.

He didn't want to leave Wellhaven. Period.

And that was it. The first little snowflake that balled into another, rolling rolling rolling, until the snowball was so big and heavy, we couldn't breathe beneath its force.

We lost sight of what once was, what we had wanted, what we had planned.

We lost sight of each other.

Everyone told us it was normal. We were high school sweethearts, married too young to know better. People fall apart. Marriages don't always last.

But still, that divorce felt like the biggest failure of my life. It felt like everything I thought could exist in this world was no longer possible, like I'd been lying to myself all along.

It crushed me.

And though River showed no emotion, I knew it crushed him, too.

After we ate dinner, I offered to take care of the dishes — mostly because I was getting more and more anxious as each moment ticked by, and I needed something to do. When I finished, I didn't know what to do with myself. Talking hadn't worked, and there was no television to turn on for the noise I desperately wished for.

It seemed River had decided to live the life of a caveman once I was gone — no Internet, no phone, no TV.

The only sound I was afforded was the storm raging on outside.

The wind whistled, the wood cabin creaked against the weight of it and perhaps the snow, too. It was so dark now that I couldn't see anything out the window, but I stared out it anyway, absentmindedly petting Moose where he lay curled up on my lap on the couch.

"Can you *please* do something?" River said after a while, and when I looked over to where he sat at one of the chairs at the folding table, he was glaring at me over the pages of the book in his hand. "You're driving me nuts with all that sighing."

I hadn't even realized I'd sighed *at all* until he called me out on it, but once he had, I realized it was all I'd been doing since I sat down.

"Well, what am I supposed to do? You don't have a television. Or Internet. And apparently having a conversation is off the table."

I could almost hear the grinding of his jaw as he turned his attention back to his book. "I've got a whole shelf of books over there."

"I don't feel like reading."

"Well, read, or don't read, I don't care. But whatever you do, be quiet about it."

I sighed, heavy and loud, just to earn myself one more glare over that book. I couldn't help it. I smirked when he looked away again.

The only light left on in the place was a tall lamp in the corner, and it cast a warm glow over half his face, leaving the rest in shadows. I wondered how he could read with the light in front of him instead of behind him, and again found myself wanting to point that out and make his life easier by advising he switch chairs, but I held back.

Partly because with the way he sat now, I could study his face.

I couldn't explain the rollercoaster of emotions I'd felt since seeing him out on the road. In fact, I wasn't sure I'd allowed myself to feel anything at all until that very moment that I watched him reading, his brows bent together, frown firmly in place like the book he was supposedly taking so much pleasure in was actually bringing him great pain.

It just felt... odd, to be there with him again. To be around a cabin full of things that smelled like him, and yet nothing like the way our home used to smell when we had one together. He was the same boy I'd loved for most of my life, and yet he wasn't a boy at all any longer.

When I blinked, he was throwing his arm around me after a baseball game, sweaty and smelly, but I leaned into him, anyway. I blinked again, and I saw him laughing under a handful of rice as we walked out of the church by the lake. Another blink, and he was holding me as I cried after burning my first attempt at my mother's chicken casserole in our new home.

Every blink, a new memory.

I was lost in those tiny specks of time until River glanced up at me, those piercing green eyes finding mine, and I tore my gaze away quickly, looking out the window again.

I wished I was home.

I was supposed to be with Mom and Dad and my little sister, Beth. I was supposed to be eating pumpkin pie and watching Christmas movies. I was supposed to be listening to Christmas music as we all sat around the tree, or drinking hot chocolate on the porch, or decorating cookies like Beth and I did as kids.

I was *not* supposed to be stuck in an old cabin with my ex.

I fought the urge to sigh again as I looked around at the utter lack of Christmas cheer. He *did* have a tree in the corner, between the fireplace and the window, but it looked like it had been placed by someone else. It was in a stand without a skirt to cover it, and it didn't have a single decoration on it — no lights, no garland, no tinsel or ornaments. And aside from that tree? There was nothing. Not a single stocking or wreath or even a freaking candy cane. The entire place was void of anything that would hint that Christmas was the day after tomorrow.

And suddenly, I had an idea.

"I know what I can do," I announced, popping off the couch. Moose lifted his head and one ear, watching me in a sleepy daze before his head rested on his paws again.

"Oh yippee, it's a Christmas miracle," River mumbled.

I rolled my eyes, walking over to stand proudly in front of him. "I'm going to decorate."

It was his turn to sigh, and he held his place in his book with one thumb before looking up at me. "Do what?"

"I'm going to decorate. You need some holiday spirit in here."

He blinked. "I don't have space for holiday spirit."

"Sure, you do. I mean, you've already got the biggest part," I said, pointing at the bare tree. "It's just sad that you have that whole tree and not a single thing on it."

River glanced at the tree with a look I couldn't decipher, and then his eyes found mine again.

"Come on," I begged. "You've got to have a box of Christmas decorations."

The heavy sigh he let loose next made me smile.

"You *do*, don't you? Where is it?"

"The loft," he said, nodding up toward the ceiling behind me. I followed his gaze and found a small, triangle loft that fit with the roof of the cabin, settled right above the bed. I wasn't sure how I'd missed it before, and I found myself wondering why he hadn't done something with it. It didn't look to be that large, at least from this angle, but it would be enough to have a small sitting area, or perhaps another bed, or a reading nook.

As it was, it was dark and ominous and not inviting in the slightest.

I turned back to him, expectant.

"Look, you can do whatever you want to do, so long as you leave me alone."

He went back to reading like I wasn't even there, and as much as I didn't love the idea of climbing up into that loft without any help, the alternative was to sit back down on the couch and stare out the window for eternity.

So, with a shrug and a *fuck it*, I got to work.

I knew River was watching me. It didn't matter that his eyes never left the pages of his book as I climbed the creaky ladder up to that loft, he was watching me. He hadn't flipped a page when I peeked down at him once I'd made it to the top, and his jaw was set like it was made of stone.

Stubborn ass.

I used the flashlight of my phone once I made it up into the loft, carefully sidestepping the massive cobwebs that cluttered the stacks of boxes until I found what I was looking for. There were two old and musty boxes falling apart and splitting at the edges, but they were both faintly labeled *Christmas*.

I smiled in victory.

At least, until I realized I had to figure out a way to get them *down* the ladder now.

I chewed my lip, lifting each box to test the weight before I looked down at the ladder, and then back at each box.

When I glanced down at River, he was looking at me, too.

"Oh, for Christ's sake," he grumbled, slamming his book down and using the table to hold his spot, just like it had been when I first walked in. Then, he stomped over to the bottom of the ladder and climbed a few rungs, holding his hands up toward me. "Hand them down."

I wanted to do a little fist pump of victory again, but knew I was testing it already, so I just silently handed down each box with a smile that River didn't return.

As soon as the boxes were on the ground, River was back at the table and his nose back in his book.

I lugged each box over closer to the tree, taking a moment to warm my hands by the fire. Moose was up and excited again, wagging his tail and sniffing the boxes. I watched him with a smile for a long moment before I opened the first one.

When I did, I lost the ability to breathe.

I'm not sure what I expected. Maybe it was to see some lights, some ornaments, some holiday trinkets from the dollar store in town. Maybe I thought I'd find some old Christmas décor that he'd rummaged from a yard sale. And maybe part of me was curious to see just *what kind* of décor he'd picked out, once he didn't have me around.

But I never expected to open that box and see all of *our* old Christmas décor staring back at me.

I glanced at River once the box was open, but he was focused on the book, and he turned the page just as my eyes found the box again. My hands trembled with my next breath, and I reached inside, pulling out each item one by one.

Our lights, the white and blue ones I'd picked out to go with the theme I'd always wanted on my tree.

Our tree skirt, navy blue with silver and white trim and a beautiful, stitched snowy scene.

Our ornaments — the silver bell my parents had given us, the Santa-hat wearing *Star Wars* figurines I'd given him as a gift our second year together because I knew it was his favorite series of all time, and even the two little reindeer, one with a bow in her hair, holding each other, with our names and wedding date written in black ink below them.

Our First Christmas.

My eyes stung with emotion I hadn't felt in years, and when I glanced back up at River, he was watching me.

"You... you kept our stuff," I said quietly, stupidly.

River's only acknowledgement was to close his book — softly, this time — and then he made his way over to where I sat by the tree. He reached inside, pulling out one of the *Star Wars* ornaments and turning it about in his hands.

I watched him for a long moment, wondering why he would have kept them. When I left, I assumed he hated me. He hadn't fought for me to stay, that was for damn sure, and he didn't show a single ounce of emotion when I brought up what I wanted, when I asked what *he* wanted, when I got so tired of waiting for an answer that I gave him an ultimatum.

Come with me...or let me leave without you.

And he chose the latter.

My next swallow was more difficult than the last, and I reached for the other box, cracking the top open with my stomach in knots over what I might find inside.

And when I saw what was on top, I gasped.

My eyes flicked to River, who watched me with his brows pinched together and frown firmly in place. I let our gazes stick for a moment before I turned my attention back to the box, pulling out the old, worn quilt on top.

"River..." I whispered, shaking my head as I pulled the fabric into my chest. I inhaled the scent, and a flurry of memories assaulted me like the snowflakes falling on the ground outside. I closed my eyes, soaking it in, and when I opened them again, they met River's. "The Christmas Blanket," I said softly, a smile spreading on my lips. "You kept the Christmas Blanket."

He swallowed, and the corner of his lips tugged up just a smidge — almost so imperceptibly that I wondered if it happened at all. Then, he shrugged, his eyes on mine.

Watching.

Waiting.

And with just that look, those emerald green pools took me back in time.

The Christmas Blanket

Ten Years Earlier

*I*was our first Christmas Eve as a married couple.

In my head, I'd always imagined what this would be like. I pictured us in our own home, with our own tree, and our own Christmas decorations. I imagined how we would decorate outside — would we put lights around the door and across the roof? Would we have a Nativity scene in the yard? What would the wreath on our door look like?

Blame it on all the fairy tales I'd read, or the fact that my parents were a real-life fairy *tale, but my imagination had run wild since I was a little girl, thinking of all the possibilities.*

Instead, River and I were in a run down, one-bedroom apartment on the east side of Wellhaven, with a busted heater and a small, sad Christmas tree that we only had thanks to the local tree-seller taking pity on us and giving us one of the rejects still left over just a few days before Christmas.

I stared at that tree from my spot on our old couch, a hand-me-down from my parents, and felt my heart ache a little. There were only two ornaments on the tree — one from my parents, a silver bell, and one from his parents, two little reindeers that said Our First Christmas *with our names and wedding date underneath it.*

I was eighteen. River was nineteen.

It'd all seemed so romantic, getting married right out of high school. River was everything I ever wanted or needed, and I didn't care that our wedding was modest, or that we didn't get to go on a honeymoon, or that we couldn't immediately buy a big house with a big yard and a big porch and a big white fence. This one-bedroom apartment was fine by me, as long as he was in it.

But now, staring at our barren tree, with my feet so cold I thought they'd fall off at any moment even wrapped up in two pairs of socks and tucked under Moose's fur where he lay at my feet on the floor, I wondered if we'd rushed it all.

Would it have been smarter to wait? What if we would have gone to college first? What if we would have saved up for a big wedding, and a long, luxurious honeymoon in the Bahamas?

And what would it be like to be in a little house, with a real Christmas tree, and real Christmas decorations?

As it was, I worked down at the supermarket in town — usually only thirty hours a week. River did odds and ends jobs whenever and wherever he could. Sometimes he was a plumber, sometimes a car mechanic, other times an electrician or lawn mower or forest clearer. If there was a job in town, River found it, and he worked it with a smile — even though I knew he was tired, and the days were long, and it wasn't what made him happy.

But he did it for us.

We saved up every penny we could after the bills were paid, but somehow, that savings would disappear no sooner than we had it saved up. The car transmission would go out, or Moose would have to go to the vet, or someone in town would go through a hard time, and we'd help in whatever way we could.

And now, it was Christmas Eve, barely above zero degrees outside with another round of snow fluttering in, and we didn't have a working heater or a fireplace or even a single strand of lights on our Christmas tree.

River sat down next to me on the couch once he was out of the shower, one that was absolutely necessary after a long day of work. He couldn't even afford to take the holiday off. I leaned into his fresh scent, his body still warm from the water. He wrapped me in his arms, and I sighed, laying my head on his chest with my eyes still on the tree.

"I wish I could jump inside that head of yours," he said after a while, rubbing my arms to keep me warm.

"Trust me. It's not fun in here."

A soft chuckle left his chest. "Talk to me."

I shook my head, leaning into him more, just wanting to be held. And River obliged me for a long while before he kissed my forehead and pulled back, still holding me, but with enough space that he could look at me, too.

"Come on. Out with it."

"You'll think I'm horrible," I said, trying to bury my face in his chest, but he held my chin to stop me.

"Try me."

I sighed, looking at the tree. "I just... I've dreamed about this for so long, what it would be like to have my first Christmas with my husband. I always pictured a beautiful tree, like the one my mom always has. All the lights and the ornaments and the candy canes. And I imagined decorating a wreath, and a yard, and baking pies all night long on Christmas Eve." My eyes welled with tears. "But here it is, Christmas Eve, and we both worked all day. We're exhausted. We don't have the money for any Christmas gifts, let alone decorations, and we're going to your parents' for breakfast and my parents' for dinner because we wouldn't have any sort of holiday meal otherwise." I sniffed. "And I'm so cold, and so sick and tired of being so cold. If we were in a house, we'd have a fireplace. But all we have is a broken heater and that small space heater in the corner that barely does a thing," I said, gesturing to the little box doing its best to fill our apartment with warm air.

My bottom lip trembled as River ran his thumb along my jaw, and I leaned into his palm, my eyes finding his.

"I don't mean it to sound ungrateful," I said. "I just… is it awful to say that I'm a little sad that this is our first Christmas Eve?"

River shook his head, a gentle smile on his lips. "I'm a little sad, too."

At that, my eyes found his. "Really?"

He nodded. "It's okay, Eliza. It's okay to be sad, to want more for us. I want more for us, too. I wish…"

He stopped, his next words seemingly strangled by emotion, and I squeezed his hand where he held me. His eyes looked longingly at the tree, and then he sighed, squeezing me once more before he stood.

"Wait here," he said.

He disappeared into the bedroom, and I wrapped myself up as much as I could in my sweater, tugging it over my knees, too. Even with a beanie on that covered my ears, I was still shivering, and I missed the warmth of River's arms around me.

When he returned, he held a large box in his hands — wrapped haphazardly in newspaper with a bow made out of shoestring. Moose hopped up and circled River with the box, trying to sniff at it.

I laughed when River sat it on the couch between us. "What is this?"

"It's your Christmas gift," he said with a shy smile. "I wanted to wait until tomorrow morning, but... well... I think tonight is better."

My heart zipped with panic. "River! We said no gifts!" I shook my head, fingers running over the paper on the box. "I didn't... I don't have one for you."

"Would you just open it, woman?"

I shook my head, pinching his side before I pulled at the first shoestring, and then the other, freeing the hold on the box. I peeled back the newspaper carefully, and then opened the box — the one that had held the space heater his dad bought for us when our heater broke.

Inside the box was a beautiful blanket.

It had the look of a quilt, with "patches" covering every inch of it, though they weren't actually stitched on. It was the pattern, but it gave the look that each little square had been *sewed and stitched together. The blanket was every shade of green and red imaginable, with little scenes playing out in each square — Santa on his sleigh, presents around a tree, baby Jesus in the manger, a snowman with a carrot nose. On and on, every square telling a story as I peeled the blanket out of the box, unfolding it as I did.*

The blanket was massive — the largest one I'd ever seen. And it was heavy, lined with fleece. I marveled at the pictures and the colors as I pulled it out, until the entire thing rested in a heap over my lap, River's, and the empty box between us.

"It's beautiful," I said with a smile, holding it to my chest. "And so warm.*"*

River smiled, setting aside the box between us and wrapping us both up in the new blanket. Its warmth was instantaneous, and it seemed to hold our body heat underneath it like a sauna. I cozied up inside it, tucking the edges under my legs and bum before leaning into River's embrace.

"I know it's not much," he said, shaking his head. "And maybe I shouldn't have spent the money I did on this blanket. I'm sure we

could have used it for something else. We need milk and bread. We're almost out of coffee. Hell, most importantly, we need another space heater while we wait for old man Lonny to fix our heat." He pulled back, tilting my chin until our eyes met. "But I wanted you to have this blanket. I wanted you to have a gift to open on Christmas, because you should, and because you deserve it." He swallowed. "You deserve so much more."

I framed his face, shaking my head, but before I could speak, he continued.

"I know this isn't what either of us pictured when we thought of our first Christmas together. God knows I wish I could give you everything you've ever dreamed of, Eliza. I wish I could give you the house and the yard and the big tree and the kitchen of your dreams. But, take this blanket as a promise. This is my promise that I will work hard, all my life, to give you everything I can. I will do everything in my power to get you that house, to shower you in gifts, to make all your dreams come true." He leaned in to press a kiss to my lips, long and slow. "And I will never stop fighting for us."

Tears flooded my eyes again, but this time from a completely different emotion. I wrapped my arms around his neck and pulled his lips to mine, kissing him over and over, again and again.

"You silly boy," I said through a mixture of laughter and tears. "You are the only gift I have ever wanted or needed. You are the best gift I have ever been given." I shook my head. "I'm sorry that I lost sight of that."

"One day, you'll have it all," he promised me.

But when I patted the spot next to us on the couch and Moose hopped up to sit on the other side of me, I wrapped that blanket around me and River a little tighter, leaning into his warm arms and feeling his lips press against my hair. And I knew one thing to be true.

"I already do."

God's Favorite Joke

$\mathcal{M}$oose licking my face brought me back to the present, and as if he had also been in that memory with me, he nuzzled into the blanket, letting out little playful snorts as he rolled around in it.

I laughed, patting his belly, my eyes tracing over the little scenes on each square just like they had all those years ago.

"I can't believe you still have this," I said, glancing up at River. His eyes were on the blanket, too, though he wore those bent brows just as fiercely as before.

He said nothing.

"I still remember when you gave it to me," I said with a smile, running my hands over the fabric. "God, I don't think I would have survived that cold Christmas without it." I chuckled. "And we used it every year after that. Do you remember? It was our tree skirt one year, if I remember right." I shook my head. "I used to love pulling it out every year, having it on the couch for us to cuddle under." My heart squeezed. "I think it's my favorite gift I've ever received."

My eyes found River's then, and he was watching me with a sort of glaze over those green irises. His Adam's apple bobbed hard in his throat.

Then, abruptly, he stood.

"I'm going to bed."

I blinked, mouth hinging open as I scrambled to my feet, too. "Wait," I started, but when he turned to look at me, I found I didn't know what else to say. I couldn't claim that it was early, since it was well after ten now, and if I knew anything about River, it was that he got up early. And I couldn't ask him to stay up and help me decorate, knowing that was the last thing he wanted to do.

But I wanted him to wait.

I just couldn't figure out why.

"You can have the bed," he said when I didn't speak. "I'll take the couch."

"You don't have to do that."

"I'm not letting you sleep on the sofa, Eliza."

I swallowed, nodding. "Okay. Thank you." Then, I chewed my lip, looking behind me at the open boxes, the Christmas Blanket spilling half out of the bigger one. "Would it keep you up if I stayed up a little while longer?" I asked, facing River again. "I really would like to decorate, if that's okay."

River's eyes flicked behind me, his jaw tense again. "You know I can sleep through a hurricane."

"Or in this case, a blizzard?" I joked.

He didn't laugh.

"Come on, Moose," he said, patting his thigh. Then, his eyes met mine. "It's too cold to take him out tonight, and there's no telling if I'd even be able to get the door open with the snow right now. I'm going to lay some newspaper out in the bathroom for him. Just let me know if he does a number two and you see it before I do."

"I can clean it up," I offered.

"No need," he said, turning his back on me. "He's my dog."

The truth of that statement stung like dry ice on a wet tongue. I watched Moose follow him back to the bathroom, and when the door closed with a *snick*, I winced as if he'd slammed it.

River got ready for bed quietly — so quietly I didn't even realize he had laid down on the couch while I'd been unpacking all the items from the two boxes. It wasn't until I turned with the Christmas Blanket draped over my arms and found him lying there, his feet hanging over the arm of one side, arm resting over his eyes on the other, that I realized he was no longer in the bathroom.

He had a blanket that only covered him from his shins to his armpits, and the pillow shoved under his head was small and not nearly as fluffy as the two he'd left for me on the bed. But by the sound of his breath, he was already asleep, and I remembered with a smile that that man could sleep anywhere, anytime, through anything.

I set the blanket aside, carefully taking the first string of lights from where I'd set it on the stone edge of the fireplace. I plugged it in, smiling when the cool blue bulbs came to life. The crackling of the fire and the quietness only fresh falling snow can bring was my only comfort as I strung those lights, and then the white ones. I wrapped the silver garland around next, and then I carefully placed each ornament.

As I decorated, my thoughts ran wild.

It was so strange, being back in this town, in this cabin, back with River. It was like the last four years of my adventures around the globe had been a dream, and I'd just woken up back in my own bed, in my own home.

Except it wasn't my home at all.

Not anymore.

But why did it feel that way? Why did I feel such warmth and comfort in the same place I'd felt so stuck in?

I found myself wondering more and more with each new piece of decoration what my life would have been like, if things would have been different. Holding that Christmas blanket, it was hard to remember the bad times. It was hard to remember the fights, the weeks of silence from River, of him not letting me in and me fighting for him to try for us.

How did we go from that pure, innocent love, to practical strangers living under the same roof?

How had he gone from the man swearing he would fight for us, to the one telling me I should go on without him?

How had *I* gone from the girl who had all she ever needed in her husband and her dog, to the woman who needed more to feed her soul than this small town could ever provide?

My mom used to always quote Woody Allen.

If you want to make God laugh, tell him about your plans.

I thought I understood that when I was a little girl. I thought even more so when I was a young woman, a young wife.

But now, thinking about the plans I'd made, the way those plans had fallen apart, the path life had led me on that I never would have imagined... I think I finally *truly* understood it.

I must have been God's favorite joke.

River let out a loud snore, and I suppressed a giggle, watching as he flopped around a few times in his attempt to turn into a more comfortable position. Moose flopped around in his own bed on the floor next to the couch in solidarity, ending up on his back with his legs spread, belly up.

River's breathing smoothed out again after a moment, heavy and steady, and I watched his chest rise and fall with each breath. In his tossing and turning, the little blanket that couldn't have been doing much anyway had wrapped around his legs, covering nothing more than one thigh and calf.

I smiled, chest aching in a most unfamiliar way as I unfolded the Christmas Blanket, spreading the massive thing over where he lay. It covered every inch from his toes to his shoulders, and I tucked it around him a little for good measure.

My throat was tight as I looked down on him — the stranger, the man I once knew better than I knew myself.

How had we lost a love that was so true?

And who were we now, on the other side of that loss?

Those questions kept me awake long after I climbed into his bed that night — into sheets that smelled like River, my head resting on pillows that I knew without looking were the ones we'd bought together.

That night, I dreamed about all the places I'd been in the last four years. I dreamed of Italy, and Canada. Of Scotland and Japan. I dreamed of the south of France and the U.S. Virgin Islands and the stunning coast of Australia. Only instead of being on the ground, I was flying over every place I'd explored, pointing at the different landmarks with an ever-extended finger.

And I wasn't flying in a plane.

I was sitting cross-legged on a magical Christmas Blanket, floating over the cities and mountains and beautiful rivers.

And there beside me, holding my free hand as I pointed out everywhere I'd been with the other, was River.

Humbug

I woke the next morning to the smell of a strong pot of coffee brewing and the sweet sound of bacon sizzling.

I reached my arms up overhead, toes pointed toward the foot of the bed, letting out a giant yawn as I stretched. When my eyes finally cracked open, I found a slobbering Moose staring at me from the side of the bed.

I chuckled, "Morning, Moose."

His tail wagged even more excitedly when I plopped my feet on the floor, and instantly, I reached for the pair of socks I'd stripped off in the middle of the night, along with my big sweater. Even with that and my sweatpants, I was freezing.

I took my time petting Moose, making sure to scratch his butt and behind his ears and under his collar like I knew he loved. Then, I looked out the window at the blinding blanket of white.

It was difficult to tell just how much snow had fallen because it was still falling — or maybe what had already fallen was just being blown around by the wind. I couldn't be sure, but it was easy to see the conditions hadn't improved much. It was cloudy and windy and there was definitely no way I was getting to my parents — at least, not anytime soon.

I made a pit stop in the bathroom, brushing my hair and my teeth before I made my way into the kitchen, rubbing my hands together.

"Hey," I said, leaning a hip against the counter. "Merry Christmas Eve."

A sort of grunt was the gist of the response I got from River, who was flipping bacon in a sizzling skillet on the stove.

Shirtless.

And somehow, he seemed to be... *sweaty?*

There was just a light sheen of gloss over his chest, his arms, his abdomen — all which were bigger than I ever remembered seeing. He'd always been more of the lean variety, thanks to years of playing baseball, but he'd filled out. The ridges of his abs were thick and cut, his biceps round and full, chest puffed without trying.

Those lean lines and edges led all the way down to where a pair of black jogger pants hung on his hips, and I'd have been blind not to see just how *well fitted* they were in certain areas.

When my eyes made their way back up to River's face, he was already looking at me.

Which meant he'd *definitely* caught me staring.

"Aren't you freezing?" I asked, crossing my arms over my chest.

I thought I saw a little smirk at the corner of his lips, but he turned back to the bacon before I could be sure. "Just worked out. Hope I didn't wake you."

"You didn't," I said, ignoring the little visions frolicking in my head at the thought of what kind of workout he'd done. Then, I walked over to the pot of coffee. "*This* did."

"Help yourself. Mugs are up there." He nodded toward one of the cabinets before taking the bacon off the skillet and setting the strips on a paper towel-covered plate. He reached into the fridge next for the carton of eggs, setting six of them on the counter and dropping the first two into the still sizzling skillet.

I added a touch of sugar to my coffee once it was poured, and as soon as I took the first sip, my chest warmed, and I sighed with relief. "Thank you," I said, tilting my mug toward him.

A nod was my only response.

For a while, I just watched him cook the eggs, heart warming a little when I realized he was making two of them scrambled, the way I liked them, while he made the rest sunny side up.

He remembered.

I sipped my coffee, wrapping my hands around the mug to soak up all the warmth I could. "You're a pretty great host for someone who wasn't expecting anyone."

A shrug.

"Did you see the tree?"

A nod.

"Well, do you *like* it?"

"I liked it just as well before."

I snorted, shaking my head. "You're such a Scrooge. Come on, you know it's pretty. You picked out half of those ornaments. And I even hung up your favorite wreath," I said, pointing to the front door. "Provided, it's on the inside when it should be on the *outside,* but at least we can see it this way."

River finished the last of the eggs, and then he served up my scrambled and a few slices of bacon on a plate and handed it to me. "I didn't make toast."

I chuckled, taking the plate. "Thank you." Then, I nudged him. "See? See how easy that is, those two simple words? You should try them sometime."

He rolled his eyes up to the ceiling before they found mine, and then he plastered on the fakest smile I'd ever seen. "Thank you, Eliza, for decorating when I didn't ask you to."

"And for doing it quietly, as requested," I added. "You're welcome."

River made a noise under his breath, piling up his own plate as we both made our way over to the table he'd been reading at the night before. The metal of the folding chair was cold, even through my sweatpants, but the coffee was still hot enough to help when I took another sip, and Moose curled up right on top of my feet to help the cause — though I was pretty sure he just wanted some bacon.

Which, of course, I slipped to him under the table when River wasn't looking.

River stopped long enough to pull on a long-sleeve thermal before joining me at the table, and I was thankful for his new muscles being covered again. I found them far too distracting — though I'd never admit that to him.

"So," I said after a stretch of silence. "What's that you're working on?"

I nodded toward the mess of saw dust and wood in the middle of the cabin over by the bookshelves.

"Boot barn," he said, shoveling a heap of eggs into his mouth. He washed it down with a big pull of coffee. "Making it for Mrs. Owens. She's giving it to her son as a wedding gift."

"I really like the color of the wood."

"Cedar."

I nodded, sipping my coffee with my eyes on the project. "So, is that what you're doing now? Woodwork?"

River shrugged. "Sometimes. More of a hobby than anything."

Of course, I thought. He'd been that way ever since I'd known him. River hated school, hated tests, hated anything that required studying or long-term dedication. He was smart as hell, and skilled, but when it came to applying himself... well... he just *didn't*. He preferred one-off projects that he could do in a day or two and be done with.

"I guess as long as it pays the bills, right?" I said.

Another shrug. "It doesn't."

I frowned. "What do you mean?"

"It's a hobby, like I said. I'm doing it as a favor to Mrs. Owens."

I shook my head. "River, you should charge for work like that. It's... I mean, the materials alone have got to be expensive."

"Mrs. Owens has done a lot for me through the years," he said, his eyes finding mine. "For *us*, if you remember."

I shut up at that, because I *did* remember. Leila Owens was the one who gave me the job down at the supermarket fresh out of high school, and she'd let me take home "expired" food more times than I could count, knowing that River and I didn't have much.

"Besides, I make plenty to cover the bills working for Skidder."

I frowned. "Skidder? I thought he said he wouldn't hire you unless you got your journeyman certificate."

"He did say that."

I blinked. "Okay, so... then... how are you working for him, exactly?"

"I got my certificate."

He said the words casually, as if it were obvious, as if that test wasn't extremely difficult and required months of studying to pass. Plus, you had to do a certain amount of hours as an apprentice on top of it.

I'd pushed him to go for it more times than I could count when we were together, and he'd dug his heels in every time, saying he didn't need a piece of paper to get by.

River picked up a piece of bacon, crunching on it while he looked at my expression with a slight amusement in his eyes.

"You... you did it? You got your journeyman's?"

He nodded.

"River... that's amazing! I mean..." I shook my head, mouth still hanging open. "I always knew you could do it, I just..."

"You never thought I actually would."

I clamped my mouth shut.

"It's okay," he said. "I never did either. But, well..." He scratched at the stubble on his jaw. "Let's just say I had time on my hands. I figured I might as well use it constructively."

A long silence passed between us, and I ate my last piece of bacon, chewing more on what he'd just told me than the meat itself.

"So, you're working for Skidder now. And what do you do?"

"A little of everything. Electrician work, plumbing, welding, carpentry... whatever he needs."

"How many hours have you put in with him so far?"

River shrugged. "Not sure. It's been about two years."

I must have looked like a trout trophy on the wall for the way my mouth was hanging open.

"I'm so proud of you," I managed to say.

River's eyes found mine, and there was something there that I couldn't quite decipher — a longing, or perhaps a deep pain disguised as longing.

I couldn't put a name to it.

All I knew was that I felt it, too.

My chest was still tight, eyes bouncing back and forth between his when he cleared his throat and scraped the last of his eggs off the plate and onto his fork, shoveling it into his mouth. "What about you?" he asked. His eyes flicked to mine, but then he shrugged, as if he didn't really care, even though he was asking. "Been seeing the world like you wanted to?"

I smiled. "Some of it, yeah."

He took a sip of his coffee, running his thumb over the handle for a moment. "What's it like?"

My rib cage squeezed painfully around my lungs. I hated the way that question sounded so defeated when it came from his lips, the way he couldn't even look at me when he asked it.

"Weird. Beautiful. Breathtaking. Awful. Incredible." I stared at my own hands. "It's hard sometimes, being alone, *traveling* alone. I've had more than my fair share of breakdowns. But..." A smile found me then. "When I'd go on a hike and reach a stunning vantage point, or talk to someone from a different culture — even through a language barrier, or taste a food I've never tasted before, or hear a new type of music I'd never heard before..." I shook my head. "It's like I can't even remember the hard times it took to get there."

My eyes found River's, and he wore a subdued smile. "What's been your favorite place so far?"

"Italy," I answered quickly. "Hands down, Italy. The food, the wine, the people, the landscape... they have it all. There's country, and beautiful coastal towns, and bustling cities." I paused, rolling my lips together before I looked at him again. "Would you maybe want to see some pictures?"

River frowned, looking down at his coffee mug even though it was empty now.

I didn't wait for an answer before I grabbed my phone off the bedside table where I'd plugged it in, pulling up my photos from Italy. I pulled my chair over next to River's, showing him the first one.

"This was in Tuscany. I stayed on this gorgeous farm with a lovely family. They let me stay for free as long as I worked."

"It's beautiful," he said as I swiped through the pictures, showing the Tuscan hills and cypress trees. "What did you do for them?"

"A little of everything, kind of like you," I said, nudging him. "I'd cook, clean, pick grapes, shake olives off the trees when the season came. I'd do the shopping in town. Sometimes, I'd babysit." I shrugged. "Whatever they asked of me."

"I can see why it's your favorite," River said, swiping through. I noticed that he paused longer on the photos I was in rather than the ones I wasn't. "You look happy."

"I am," I whispered.

River swallowed, handing the phone back to me.

"Want to see more?"

His frown was so severe, you would have thought I'd just asked him to make the choice between sticking a fork through his arm or his leg. But his eyes found mine, and he nodded — just once.

What was left of my coffee grew cold as I showed him album after album, picture after picture on my phone. I told him stories of the families I'd stayed with, the crews I'd worked with, the houses I'd watched over in exchange for a place to stay, the hostels that had creeped me out more than once, and even the time I slept in an open field in the south of France because of a transportation mishap.

I showed him pictures of castles and reefs, of skyscrapers and beaches, of hidden hiking trails and bustling bars.

And with each new story *I* told, I asked him for one of his own.

I wanted to know how he spent his free time, to which he answered with a multitude of things that surprised me. He'd fallen in love with reading, and fishing, and he'd even picked up skiing, though he said he was still figuring it out. He was trying to teach himself another language and had decided on Mandarin, mostly because everyone said it was one of the most difficult to learn.

And I wanted to know about our friends, the ones who weren't on social media. He filled me in on how everyone around town was doing, the drama and the gossip — well, as much gossip as River would partake in, anyway.

It wasn't a lot of talking, and sometimes we'd have long stretches of silence between us. But it felt good to talk at all, to ask questions and actually get responses.

To be asked questions in return.

At one point, I even called him on it. *See? Isn't this nice?* To which I received nothing more than a wry smile before he turned the attention back to one of my stories.

"And how are your mom and dad?" I asked after maybe an hour had passed.

The second the question left my lips, River went stiff.

I frowned. "I... I haven't heard from them in a while. We kept in touch for about a year after I left. You know, talking on the phone here and there. But then they stopped calling, and stopped answering my calls..."

There was a coldness in his eyes, and they seemed to lose focus where they were trained on my phone screen.

"I just figured they were trying to put some space between us... with you and me being divorced and all..."

River hastily handed my phone back to me then, abandoning his place where he'd been looking through my pictures at an old fishing port in Israel. He stood just as quickly, the legs of his chair scraping against the wood.

"River?" I asked, but he ignored me, picking up his plate and then mine. He took them to the sink and flipped the faucet on to wash, and I stood to join him. "Did I say something wrong?"

"They're dead, Eliza!" River screamed suddenly, his chest heaving when he turned his manic gaze on me. Then, he winced, pinching the bridge of his nose with his wet, soapy fingers. He blew out a breath, shaking his head before he looked at me again. "That's it," he said, quiet again. "That's how they're doing. Alright?"

If my mouth had hung open wide when he'd told me about his job with Skidder, it might as well have been a train tunnel now.

"I..." I swallowed. "I had no idea." I shook my head, eyes glossing over. "What happened?"

River sniffed, turning back to the dishes in the sink. "Dad got sick. And after he died, Mom just couldn't live without him. She was gone seven months later."

My eyes stung more, the tears welling up and falling over before I could stop them. I covered my mouth with my hands, shaking my head over and over. *How? How could this have happened?* When *did it happen?*

Why didn't my parents tell me?

Why didn't River *tell me?*

I opened my mouth to ask him just that when he held up a hand, silencing me. "Please, Eliza. Can we just..." He swallowed, hands bracing on the edge of the sink, eyes averted.

And I knew what he was asking without him having to say it.

I nodded, even though he wasn't looking at me, and then grabbed our coffee mugs off the table. I walked over to him slowly, like he was a bear caught in a trap, one that I might provoke into murdering me if I moved too quickly. I dropped the mugs in the soapy water, and then I grabbed the towel hanging on the stove.

"I'll dry," I whispered.

A Little Rum Never Hurt

The rest of the morning and afternoon, we were quiet.

I did my best to stay out of River's way. He turned on his small radio long enough to tune into the weather report — which essentially said conditions were still terrible and to stay inside. They did predict that the wind would die down overnight, and that the snow would stop falling — both of which meant I might still be able to be home on Christmas.

But only time would tell.

Once he shut the radio off, River busied himself around the house. He worked on the boot barn, read a little, played with Moose —

all while not saying anything to me. And for once, I didn't push him. I suffered my boredom in silence, even picking up a book off his shelf just to keep myself busy, and even playing a few games of solitaire.

I felt awful for what I'd asked.

It was a harmless question, or so I thought, to ask about his parents. But I'd never expected his answer to be that they were no longer with us.

Dawn and Cole Jensen may have just been my in-laws in technicality, but for all intents and purposes, they were just like my real parents.

Sure, Dawn was sassier than my mother, with her fiery auburn hair and *can't tell me shit* attitude. And Cole was broody and severe compared to my warm-hearted father. But they'd brought me up just as much as my own parents. I'd stayed as many nights in their home as I had my own in the years between when I was sixteen and eighteen, and even well after River and I had moved in together.

Dawn and River had a good relationship, but the whole town knew that River was closer with his father.

Dawn had battled with drugs for many years, and though she'd found her way out, it was during that time that River and Cole grew to be inseparable. Cole kept River focused on school, even when he didn't want to be. And River kept Cole strong, even when he didn't want to be.

They were a team, through and through, and if I knew one thing about my ex-husband, it was that no one in this world mattered more to him than his father.

Which meant it must have killed him when Cole passed.

And then to have Dawn go just as quickly...

My stomach was sour all day at the thought of it, and I couldn't *release* the thought of it. All I could think about were the memories of the times we'd all shared together, the stories River had told me about his childhood, the way Dawn and Cole had helped us as newlyweds just as much as they could manage. I thought about how fiercely they loved their son, and me by proxy.

And I thought about our last conversation, a phone call that was quick and shallow and cut short by me needing to catch a train.

I didn't know that would be my last memory of them.

I didn't know those would be the last words we ever spoke.

The cabin felt heavy and dark all day long, regardless of the Christmas cheer I'd tried to bring in with the decorations the night before. Even when I stared at that tree and hummed Christmas music to myself, I couldn't shake it.

It felt like a funeral years too late.

Maybe that's why I was exhausted by the time the sun set, and I wondered if I should just go to bed and get this day over with so I could wake up on a new one. I was just about to concede to that notion when a low hum reverberated through the cabin, and the lights flickered before cutting out altogether.

The kind of silence that engulfed us was all-encompassing.

It was almost like a blanket, the way it fell on us, heavy and thick. It lasted for a split second that seemed to stretch on for hours before Moose's nails clicked and clacked on the wood. He barked for good measure, as if we didn't already realize there was something going on.

"Shit," River mumbled under his breath. He'd been reading at the table, and thanks to the little bit of light the fire was still giving off, I could see his frown as he closed his book.

"Power's out?"

"Seems like it." He let out a long sigh. "Can't say I'm surprised. If anything, I'm shocked we didn't lose it last night with the wind. I've got some candles and flashlights... just have to *find* them—AH, SHIT!"

There was a loud thump preceding his curse, and I shot upright from where I'd been reclining on the couch, looking over my shoulder where he was by the bed now. "Are you alright?"

"I'm fine," he grumbled. "Just took a few centimeters off my big toe."

I tried not to laugh, thankful that my smile was at least covered by the semi-darkness.

A few seconds later, the cabin came more into view, thanks to a little ray of light coming from a small flashlight in River's hands. He handed me one, too, and then he started pulling out candles, setting them up in various corners of the cabin and sparking them to life.

Once they were all lit, he turned out his flashlight, and I did the same.

"Well, this is kind of cozy," I said with a smile.

River chuckled. "Always finding the silver lining."

"More of a golden glow this time."

He returned my smile for a split second before making his way back to the table, and he opened his book where he'd left off, positioning himself near a candle for more light.

I watched him reading for a while, the light and shadows playing over his face the way they had the night before. Only this time, they did a sort of dance, the flickering flames waltzing with the darkness.

I'd been so ready to pass out before. But now, with a fresh shot of adrenaline, I found my boredom suffocating and my need to do *something*, anything, growing too much to bear.

"It's Christmas Eve," I said, popping up onto my knees and draping my arms over the back of the couch. "We should do something."

"Like what?"

I frowned, because we couldn't watch a Christmas movie since he didn't have a TV, and he didn't have any games other than the ones we could play with a deck of cards. "How about we turn on the radio?" I suggested. "Find a station that's playing Christmas music. And we can bake cookies!"

"We can't bake anything," River corrected, eyes still on his book. "Power's out, dum-dum."

I threw the little pillow on the couch at him. "Hey!"

He chuckled, catching the pillow with ease and tucking it under his arm before he shut his book and looked at me with a sigh. "Just pointing out the facts. Plus, I don't have the ingredients to make cookies."

I narrowed my eyes. "*Fine*. No cookies." I paused. "What *do* you have that we could make good use of?"

River let out another long breath, but then something of a glint found his eyes, and he smirked. "I have eggnog," he said. "And rum."

A smile curled on my own lips. "Anddd Christmas music?"

River groaned but stood in concession. "Fine. But if Mariah Carey comes on, I'm throwing this radio across the room."

"Or we could just turn it off for a few minutes."

"Deal."

I jumped up off the couch, squealing with delight. The excitement had Moose up and bouncing around my legs, too, and River chuckled when we both slid into the kitchen Tom Cruise style.

"Oh, I hope they play 'The Christmas Song'. It's my favorite!"

River shook his head, pulling down two glasses from the cabinet with another grunt of annoyance.

But I saw the smile he was trying to fight.

The Why's and the Why Not's

"That's so not true!" I said on the heels of a hiccup, giggling at the sound of it. "It was *you* who dared me to get on that old rope swing in the first place."

"Oh, like you wouldn't have done it whether I dared you or not," River argued. "That's why you wanted to party out behind that old house. It's why you dragged us all there that day. You wanted to get on that rope swing, and you know it." He shrugged then, taking a drink of his eggnog that was *definitely* more rum than anything at this point. "Not my fault you didn't realize the rope was rotted."

"I had a bruised tailbone for *weeks*," I reminded him. "And you, you just laughed at me. Asshole."

"It *was* funny!"

"I hurt myself!"

"You survived. And trust me, if you could have seen the way your arms flailed when that rope broke, sending you into the water right there off the shore, and the way you flopped into the shallow water like a fish..." He started laughing again at the memory of it, so much so that he couldn't speak for a long moment, and I took the cinnamon stick out of my eggnog and chucked it at his head.

That made him laugh harder.

"And the sound you made," he said when he finally caught his breath. "Sounded like a cat in heat."

I joined in his laughter then, because even though I did hurt myself that day, I'd dragged us and a group of our friends down to the lake to party, it *was* pretty funny afterward.

"Wasn't that the same day that Jenny tried to dare you to kiss Tabatha?" I asked, squinting through the rum haze swimming in my head as I tried to remember.

"Oh, shit," River said on a chuckle, then he let out a low whistle. "Sure was. You were *not* happy about that."

"Hell no, I wasn't. That little tramp, she knew exactly what she was doing. Tabatha had the hots for you all through high school. She never did care that we were together." I shook my head. "Just waiting for her chance."

"Well, you didn't let her take that chance, if I remember correctly," River said with a shit-eating grin. "Because I'm pretty sure you said something along the lines of *in your dreams, Flabby Tabby* and then you straddled me and made out with me right there for everyone to see."

I smiled proudly. "Had to remind those girls who had your heart."

River's eyes crinkled more with his grin, and maybe a little from the rum, too. I'd lost count of how many spiked eggnogs we'd had. All I knew was that they had gone from a nice, smooth, proper mixture, to something closer to all rum with a splash of nog on top.

I took a drink from my glass, still smiling at the memory. Then, an idea struck me.

"We should play now."

KANDI STEINER

River cocked a brow. "Play what?"

"Truth or dare."

His smile turned into a frown, and he looked down at what remained in his glass, finishing it off before standing. He was already heading to the kitchen to refill when he said, "Aren't we a little old for games?"

"Age is just a number," I argued, hopping up from where I'd been sitting crisscross on the floor. I drained what was left of my own nog in the name of refilling at the same time as River, though he'd had a sip left in his and I'd had half a glass.

He smirked at me when I slid my glass next to his just as he was pouring the rum.

"Come on," I insisted. "It'll be fun. And tell you what — I'll even give you a skip. If I ask you something you don't want to answer, or dare you to do something you don't want to do, you can use it."

A heavy breath came from his throat as he poured.

"Pleeeease," I added, batting my lashes.

He peeked at me with a grin, and then shook his head. "Fine. But I want two skips."

"Baby."

"Hey, I just know how dirty you can play this game, and I'm not trying to go streaking in a snowstorm."

"Aw, dang it — you took my first idea!" I winked with the joke, pulling the eggnog from the fridge to top off our glasses.

Once we had our refills, we sat back down in front of the fire on the pillows we'd laid out there, and Moose curled up beside me again, wagging his tail gently when I rubbed the fur on his neck.

"Okay, truth or dare?" I asked when we were settled.

River laughed. "You're so excited. You look like a kid who just got turned loose in Disneyland."

"Answer the question."

Another laugh. "Truth."

"Lame," I teased, but then I tapped my chin, looking up to the ceiling as I thought of a question. "Oh! I know." I pointed my finger at his chest. "That one day that I walked in on you in our bedroom and you were all out of breath and naked, had you really just finished a workout and you were getting in the shower, or were you masturbating?"

His eyes went wide as saucers, and he barked out a laugh. "I can't believe you remember that."

"Answer the question, mister."

"Both."

I arched a brow. "Both?"

"I *had* just worked out. And I *was* getting in the shower," he said, smirking. "But I also might have had a little one-on-one time in-between those two things."

"I knew it!" I giggled. "You were so jumpy when I walked in. Also, no fair, didn't invite me to the party." I stuck my bottom lip out in a pout.

River just laughed me off, taking a big drink of his nog. "Your turn. Truth or dare?"

"Dare."

He shook his head like he already knew. Then, after a long pause, he said, "I dare you to take a shot."

"Done."

"Of gin."

At that, I grimaced. "Riverrrrr...noooo."

"Does that mean you're using your pass?"

I narrowed my eyes, determined when I stood. "Hell no. Pour the shot, big boy."

He did, and I took it, and promptly had to cover my mouth and squeeze my eyes shut to avoid vomiting. Once the terrible liquid had settled in my gut, I chased it with some water and a little eggnog before it was River's turn again.

This time, he chose dare.

"I dare you to stick your bare ass to that window and hold it there for sixty seconds," I said, pointing to the window on the other side of the Christmas tree. Sure, it was dark. And sure, no one lived close enough on either side of River's cabin that anyone would see.

But I knew that window was freezing cold.

River groaned, looking up to the ceiling.

"You can pass," I teased. "If you're too chicken."

"You wish," he said, and then he hopped up off the floor, and without another ounce of hesitation, he yanked his sweatpants and boxers down in one strong pull.

"River!" I said, laughing as I shielded my eyes.

"Just doing my dare."

I laughed again, shaking my head, and I swear I only peeked a little through the slits of my fingers as he walked away from me, watching each glorious muscle of his toned ass move with him.

When he got to the window, he turned to face me, using his hands to shield his member. "Alright, you can look, ya big baby." He chuckled. "Not like you haven't seen it before."

I rolled my eyes once they were uncovered, and then with a deep breath, River leaned back until his ass was on the window.

He sucked in a breath, eyes shooting open wide. "*Fuck me,* that's cold!"

I cackled, and that laughter stayed with me for the whole sixty seconds as he bounced a little, squeezing his eyes closed, cursing over and over, all the while holding his junk and pressing his ass against that window.

I may have counted slower than necessary, but once I hit sixty, he hopped back over to his pants and pulled them on quickly while I looked away, keeping my eyes on my eggnog, instead.

"That was just cruel," he said when he was clothed again, standing and holding his butt toward the fire. "Laugh while you can, because I'm going to get you back. Truth or dare?"

"Truth."

He glared at me. "Now who's chicken shit?"

I stuck my tongue out, sipping on my eggnog while I waited for him to ask his question.

"Alright," he said, plopping down in front of me on the floor again. "How many people have you slept with?"

My jaw hinged open. I waited for him to make a comment, or laugh, but he just watched me unflinchingly, waiting.

I could have used my skip. Part of me *wanted* to use my skip. But I had no idea what the rest of this game would hold, and I had a feeling I should hold onto those passes for something worse.

I swallowed. "One."

River's gaze didn't change. His forest eyes held mine until I could no longer stand the way he stared at me, the way he was looking through my answer like there was something more behind it.

No, I hadn't slept with anyone else.

No, it didn't mean anything.

Other than I had been too busy seeing the world to care about hooking up with anyone.

I cleared my throat. "Truth or dare?"

"Dare," he croaked out. "And just in case you're wondering, it's one for me, too."

My heart thumped hard in my chest at his admission, at the truth he answered that I didn't ask but wanted so desperately to know.

All this time... and he hadn't slept with anyone else, either.

What did that mean?

I lifted my eggnog to my lips, telling myself sternly that it meant *nothing*. Nothing that I needed to read into, anyway.

I tore my eyes from River's and looked at the fire, instead.

And so the game went.

I dared him to take a shot of whiskey, he dared me to lick one of Moose's dog toys. I asked him where the strangest place he'd ever peed was, and he asked me to tell him the truth about the expensive bracelet I'd come home with when we were nineteen that he knew I couldn't afford.

The more the game went on, the more we drank, and laughed, and teased each other. It seemed the harsh environment we'd lived in for the majority of the day was finally gone, and I much preferred the one we were in now.

It was close to midnight when River selected dare, and I was running out of ideas. But one glance across the room and that all changed.

"Remember that home video your dad showed me where you had that big blanket wrapped around you as a kid, and you were prancing around saying *Look at me, Dad! I'm a queen! I'm a queen!*"

"Men can't be queens, son. Men are kings." He mocked in his father's voice.

"But... boys can be queens too, right? I wanna be a queen!" I said, and we both laughed.

When the sound faded, River had a distant look in his eyes, his thumb tracing the lip of his glass.

"Alright. That's your dare," I said, snapping my fingers before the moment became too heavy. "I want a replay."

I hopped up from where I'd been sitting and grabbed the Christmas Blanket, tossing it at him. He caught it with a dramatic *oof*, folding the fabric over in his hands with a grin.

"Come on," I said, and I took a seat on the couch like I was in the audience, and the space in front of the fireplace was his stage. "Let's see it."

River heaved a sigh, but when he was up on his feet, he slipped right into the role. He held his head high, wrapping the blanket around his shoulders and letting it trail behind him while he waltzed around saying *I'm a queen! I'm a queen!*

I laughed and laughed until my sides hurt, rolling around on the couch. When River finally stopped, he stood in front of the fire with the blanket still on his shoulders, watching me.

The fire illuminated him from behind, making him something of a silhouette. I wished the power was on for the simple fact that I would have loved to see him in the twinkle of the lights winding around the Christmas tree.

Still, the garland and ornaments reflected the flames of the fire, and all the candles that surrounded us cast him in a warm glow. I watched a million different emotions pass over that half-shadowed face of his before he opened his arms, the blanket stretching out like a cape.

"Come here."

I frowned, and didn't move an inch, not until River smirked and nodded his head, motioning for me to join him.

"Come on, Eliza. Get in here."

My chest tightened when he said my name, along with my throat, and I tried but failed to swallow as I made my way over to where he stood. When I was a few feet in front of him, he grinned wider, wrapping his arms around me and pulling me flush against him.

The Christmas Blanket was around us both now, covering us in warmth. For a moment, I didn't know what to do with my hands. My arms were glued to my sides awkwardly until River chuckled, using his own hands to guide mine up to his shoulders.

Then, he wrapped his around me once more, and we started to sway.

The music from the radio had been so soft before, and us so loud, that I didn't really remember it was playing at all. But now that we were silent, it was all I heard, the smooth melody and sweet voice of Bing Crosby singing "I'll Be Home for Christmas."

We swayed gently in front of the fire, my eyes on River's chest, but I knew his were on me. I didn't know why I was so nervous, but when I finally looked up and into his eyes, I felt it ten-fold.

"Truth or dare?"

The question was just above a whisper, and I whispered my reply. "Truth."

"Do you hate me?"

I frowned, dropping my head down to his chest and soaking in the feel of his arms around me for a long while. I'd forgotten what it felt like, to be wrapped up this way, to be held. I forgot the way my head fit just perfectly under his chin, the way his flannel shirt smelled, the way I could always faintly hear his heartbeat when I rested my head on his chest like I did now.

"No," I finally said. I lifted my head again to look at him. "But sometimes, I wish I did."

His jaw tensed, but he never stopped holding me, never stopped swaying.

God, those eyes. How they'd haunted me since the last time I saw them, watching me leave in my rearview mirror. They watched me the same way now — like I was all River had ever known, all he'd ever needed, and also the only thing to ever break him.

River's hands were warm against my lower back, my hips, and he pulled me in even closer, gazing down at me over his nose.

His eyes flicked to my lips, and the breath that came from his chest when he did was one I knew I'd hear forever replayed in my memory.

Longing.

Pain.

Regret.

"Truth or dare?" I asked, voice cracking with the question.

"Truth."

"Did you ever miss me, after I left?"

He shook his head, the muscles of his jaw ticking, nose flaring, hands still pulling me in, closer, closer.

"Only every day, Eliza," he whispered, his brows bending together. "Every hour. Every minute. Every second you've been gone."

Emotion surged through me, but I didn't have the chance to break beneath it before the blanket dropped from around us, and River took me full in his arms.

And then his mouth was on mine, hard and punishing, a kiss and a gunshot all the same.

I cried out at the connection — a sigh, perhaps, or a moan or a whimper. Maybe it was all of those things, all wrapped into one, my body and brain so confused it couldn't decide how to react.

But I leaned into him, into that kiss, and the ghost that was River Jensen.

His arms were sturdy where they held me, and as our lips melded together, it was as if there was no other place in the world we could possibly be. It was a kiss we'd shared a hundred times before. It was a kiss I'd never experienced, never even *dreamed* of, not until the moment his lips were on mine. It was years of love and passion. It was years of heartache and pain. It was everything I hated, everything I desired, everything I'd forgotten and everything I would always remember, too.

This is my husband, my heart screamed. *This is the love of my life.*

This is a stranger, my brain combatted. *This is the man who let you go.*

River swept his tongue over mine, sending a bolt of electricity ripping through me, shooting straight to my core. And in the next breath, I pressed my hands into his chest, shoving him away.

I'd already turned my back when River groaned at the loss, covering my mouth with both hands. I shook my head, eyes welling with tears, emotion swimming with the alcohol in my bloodstream, making for a dangerous current I knew had the power to sweep me under.

"Why," I asked softly, almost so soft I wondered if he'd heard me at all. I turned to face him again, slowly, timidly, the glow of him blurred through my tears. "Why would you do that? Hold me like that, *kiss* me like that..." I sniffed. "But you just let me go. When I stood in front of you just like this and asked you what you wanted, what you needed. When I asked you to come with me, but you wouldn't." I shook my head, desperation aching through me. "*Why,* River?"

"Eliza..."

"Just tell me *why*."

He swallowed, his Adam's apple bobbing hard in his throat as he looked into the fire. Tears glossed his own eyes, and when he found my gaze again, I swore the way he looked at me would break whatever part of me was still holding on.

"I knew Dad was dying," he said gruffly. "He told me."

My bottom lip trembled. "What? Why didn't you tell *me*?"

"I was going to," he said. "Of course, I was going to. You were my best friend, Eliza. But I came home, and there you were, sitting at our dining table with all these plans laid out."

He shook his head, and realization washed over me like an icy flood.

It was the night I told him I wanted to leave.

Or rather, I wanted *us* to leave.

I'd spent my day off clipping photos out of travel magazines, making vision boards, planning routes and researching what we could do to earn money in each place I wanted to visit around the world. I had a plan, a way to make it work, a way for us to see the world and make enough to live on, too.

And when he walked through the door that night, it was all I could do to wait until he'd taken his coat off to tell him all of it.

"When I saw it all, and listened to you talking about getting away, about how this town was suffocating you, how you felt stuck..." He grimaced. "Eliza, I couldn't tell you. Not then."

"But you should have," I argued. "I... I could have stayed. I *would* have stayed."

"And that's exactly the problem!" River held his hands out toward me before letting them fall. "Don't you see? My dad was already dying. And if you would have stayed, you would have died, too. This town was killing you. *I* was killing you — your spirit, your dreams, your love and vivaciousness for life. I was holding you back from where you wanted to be... from *who* you wanted to be."

I shook my head, over and over, the tears falling harder now. "You should have told me. You should have given me a choice. You... you didn't fight for me," I said through my tears. "You just let me go."

"And I regret that mistake," he said firmly, his feet carrying him toward me. I wanted to move. *God*, how I wanted to back away, but I was rooted in place. "I have every minute since the one where I lost you. But I loved you, Eliza," River croaked when he was just inches from me. "I loved you. So I let you go." His hands reached out, framing my face, his eyes searching mine as he shook his head like every word was the most horrible truth. "And damn it if I don't love you still."

The next sob that broke through my chest was cut off when his mouth met mine again, this time warm and comforting and gentle, yet sure. His hands held my face, fingers curling in my hair, thumbs brushing my temples. I leaned into that touch, into that kiss, into that man with everything that I was, with everything I ever had be.

And in that moment, I was home.

It was a dizzy blur, the steps we took through the cabin to where the bed lay hidden in the shadows in the corner. The candlelight was dimmer here, the whole world seeming to turn its lights down to hum a distant *shhh*, giving us privacy and peace.

River only broke our kiss long enough to strip my sweater overhead, my hair tumbling out of the neck hole in a waterfall down my back.

Chills raced from the cool air, from the feel of his hands on me, wrapping around my rib cage in a gentle squeeze before he moved for my sports bra next. He pulled it up and over my head, too, letting it fall to the floor.

His shirt came next, and then his briefs, his sweatpants, until he was fully naked and trembling in my grasp as he backed me up to the bed.

My back hit the quilt, the fabric cold against my hot skin, but that sensation was dull compared to the way my heart raced at the sight of River standing over me. He towered like a god, peeling my sweatpants off my hips, off one leg and then the other. His eyes didn't leave mine as he did the same with my thong, and only when I was nude did he let his gaze rake over me.

I felt those eyes like big, calloused hands, working their way over my breasts, my navel, my thighs, and the little gap between them where I was already wet and throbbing for him. River's throat was so tight I heard his next swallow, and a gentle shake of his head was all I got before he was climbing on top of me, maneuvering me up until my head was on the pillow and he was between my legs.

We both shuddered at the rush of heat from our bodies being together again, and River swept my hair from my face, kissing my jaw, my neck, my collarbone and back up until his mouth claimed mine.

There was no time to think, no time to second guess or let logic sneak its way in before River was balancing all his weight on one elbow, his other hand reaching down to hook my leg up his thigh. He pressed more weight into his knees, the tip of him sliding against my wet, warm entrance in a skating glide that had us both hissing with need.

I knew the feel of him, even after all these years. I knew the shape of his crown, the lean of his shaft, the exact lining of the vein that rippled up from his base. I knew how he would fill me even before he did, but when the flex of his hips brought us together, when he slipped inside me for the first time in four trips around the sun, I gasped, holding onto that breath like it was my last.

It was a searing fire, the way he stretched me, and yet it filled me with a current of pleasure all the same. I whimpered into his mouth and he caught that cry with a growl, with a demanding kiss, with a slight withdrawal before he rocked into me again, deeper.

My other leg lifted, ankles hooking behind him, hips bucking up to give him better access. I thought I felt those lips of his curl into a smile against mine before he slid into me again, harder this time, deeper still, and he picked up the pace, finding a rhythm.

Our bodies were slick where they met, my breasts sliding against his chest as he wrapped his arms up and under my back, hooking his hands on my shoulders. He held me there as he flexed again, and I felt the muscles of his ass working under my heels with every new thrust.

It couldn't have even been a full minute of us being connected, and already, I was ready to fall apart.

But River flipped us, quickly, holding me to him to keep the connection. I unhooked my ankles just in time to land straddling him, and he sat up, back against the headboard, me in his lap.

His hands traced a trail down my shoulders, my arms, my hips, until he was grabbing my ass and helping me ride him. It didn't matter how long had passed since we last touched, he still knew every way to please me.

He knew grabbing my ass like that, tilting his hips the way he was — it was in just the right way for my clit to catch the friction it so desperately wished for. He knew that when he yanked on me hard and my hands flew forward, finding the headboard on either side of him, it was the perfect angle to let that gentled curve of his cock reach all the right spots. And he knew when he leaned forward just enough to capture my left nipple in his mouth, sucking it between his teeth, that it was all I needed to combust.

I was wild in that moment, my hips bucking uncontrollably, thighs barely even moving me up and down anymore. Now, I rocked back and forth, feeling him deep, rubbing my clit until my orgasm caught light like a dying star. It ripped me apart from the inside out, shredding me inch by inch in the most ecstasy-filled demise.

I rode every wave of that death until I was spent, limp in his arms, heaving each new breath as if it took everything I had left in me just to give my body oxygen.

River slowed his pace, kissing my lips hard, bruisingly, until he dragged those lips and nipping teeth and sweeping tongue down my neck again. I was so limp and small in his arms that it didn't take much effort for him to flip me over again, onto my stomach, with my ass in the air just the way I knew he liked it.

He slapped my ass as a reward for remembering, and I fisted my hands in the sheets as he lined up at my entrance, remembering all too well how deep he felt in this position. His hands slipped between the folds where my thighs met my hips, and in one full thrust, he filled me again.

"*Fuck*, Eliza," he husked, slipping out just to slide back in again. "So wet. So fucking *tight*."

He flexed in, again and again, picking up speed and groaning more with every new thrust. His hand splayed on my back, pushing me down even more into the sheets, and then he was riding me like a fucking horse, plowing into me. I cried out against the pain, but it was met with a searing pleasure that confused my senses.

I wanted to beg him to stop.

I wanted to beg him to *never* stop.

I didn't have the chance to decide before he was ripping out of me, the loss so violent I shuddered beneath him, and then I felt his warm release painting my ass, my back, my shoulders and my thighs all at once.

I looked over my shoulder, watching him stroking his long, thick length as the last of his release pulsed out. It was the hottest fucking thing I'd ever seen, and I knew before we'd even cleaned up that it wouldn't be the last time I'd make that man come for me tonight.

If it was up to me, that night would have lasted forever.

If it was up to me, the morning would have never come.

But it wasn't up to me.

And when the sun finally found its way through those cabin windows, bright and blinding off the snow covering the ground outside, it would be the wake-up call I never wanted.

Hangover

My head pounded me to consciousness the next morning, eyeballs throbbing beneath my lids until I was brave enough to creak them open.

I groaned when the first little ray of sunlight found me...and realized two things at the same time.

One, I was extremely warm — thanks to being sandwiched between Moose and River on the bed. Moose was on top of the quilt and River was underneath the sheets with me, his legs and arms tangled up with mine, our naked bodies stuck together and steaming.

Two, I was going to vomit.

I nearly fell on my face in my scramble out of the bed, twisting and turning until I freed each limb from the sheets. Moose barked at the commotion, and River groaned, mumbling something under his breath that sounded like *are you okay*, but I couldn't be sure, because I had approximately four seconds to get to the bathroom.

I made it to the toilet just in time to drop to my knees and forfeit whatever I had left in my stomach, which wasn't much else than booze. We'd eaten dinner so early, and then proceeded to get rip-roaring wasted the rest of the night, and my body was reminding me of those dire choices in every possible way this morning.

A long groan left me when I'd finished heaving, and I rested my cheek on the toilet, peeking up at the mass of man staring down at me.

River smiled. "Merry Christmas."

"I hate you for making me take that shot of gin."

He chuckled, lowering down to the ground next to me. It was then that I noticed the glass of something cloudy and orange in his hand, and two little candy-coated pills.

"Advil," he explained. "And chase it with this."

"What is it," I asked, sitting up and taking the glass from him, inspecting the contents.

"My hangover cure."

I arched a brow.

"Just trust me," he insisted, and so I did, tossing the pills into my mouth and washing them down with the cure. It tasted like orange juice and saltwater, and I grimaced, choking down as much as I could manage before I gave up.

When I looked back at River, at the way his eyes were crawling over me, the way his lips were set in a soft smile, I realized what I'd somehow forgotten.

I was stark ass naked.

"God, look at me," I said, curling in on myself. "A mess on Jesus's birthday."

River barked out a laugh, standing before he helped me up and back to the bed. We crawled in together, right next to a very happy Moose, who promptly licked my face in greeting.

Littered around the cabin was all the evidence of what had transpired last night. There were our half-empty glasses of spiked eggnog, and the two empty shot glasses we'd used to do our dares. The Christmas Blanket was in a heap by the fire, which had gone out overnight, and all the candles had burned down, or maybe River had blown them out.

The little radio still played Christmas music softly, and with just one look out the window, I could see the storm was over. It was still mostly cloudy, but the sun was shining through the silvery clouds.

My stomach was still unsettled when I looked at River, who had his head propped on his bicep, his eyes on me.

"So…" he said.

"So…" I echoed.

"We should probably talk."

I swallowed. "About?"

A short laugh through his nose told me he saw right through me. "Well… after last night…" He shrugged. "I think we should maybe talk about what happens next. About what this means."

Those words snapped me back to reality, and I sat up straighter in the bed, pulling the sheets up to cover my chest. I felt the panic zipping through me like live wires under my skin, and I took a deep breath to soothe my soul as best I could.

River sat up, too, watching me with bent brows now. "Eliza," he said, not really as a question so much as a warning.

"Well…" I finally said, cheeks heating. "We… we had fun. We had a good night." I paused. "Does it really have to *mean* anything?"

Even as the words formed on my tongue, I knew they were all wrong. But it was too late. I'd said them, and they hadn't hung in the space between us for longer than a second before River rolled over onto his back, eyes on the ceiling and a short puff of a laugh from his chest.

"Of course."

He shot up out of the bed before I could reach to stop him.

"I should have seen this coming," he said, more to himself than to me. He shook his head, ripping open the top drawer of his dresser. He yanked on a fresh pair of boxer briefs, and then stomped into a pair of long johns. "Lucky for you, looks like it stopped snowing. We should have you out of here and on your way by lunch."

He was already pulling on more clothing when my jaw fell open, and I watched the muscles of his back, blinking and trying to see my way out of the haze still pounding through my head. "Wait," I tried, squeezing my eyes shut. "I didn't mean it like that."

When I opened my eyes again, River was still getting dressed.

"I just... I mean..." Every word I wanted to say was scrambled, and I found myself more and more confused as I tried to explain what I felt.

What *did* I feel?

"I'm leaving," I reminded him. "I just... I came to surprise my family for Christmas, but I have a house-sitting job lined up in Corfu. And you..."

River stood straight after pulling socks on, his boots in his hands and his eyes landing hard on mine. "And I'm staying here. In boring Wellhaven," he added, shaking his head before he gave me his back. "Where nothing that matters to you lives."

My head snapped back as if he'd slapped me, and I rolled out of bed, wrapping the sheets around me. "Would you stop putting words in my mouth? You're not even letting me speak."

River spun on me. "Well, what could you possibly have to say that I'd want to hear right now, Eliza, if not that you're back, you're staying, and you want me?"

His chest puffed, up and down, his brows bent severely as he waited for me to respond.

I swallowed, trying to take a tentative step toward him, but as soon as I did, he backed away.

"Why is that the only option?" I asked softly.

I didn't get the chance to get another word out before he scoffed, turning on me again and stomping toward the door. He yanked his coat off the rack, pulling it on one arm at a time.

"You're such a stubborn ass!" I screamed, following him. "We were drunk. *Wasted*, okay? And... and..." I lost steam, waving my hand around, because the truth was that I didn't know what to say about last night.

Had we been drunk? Yes.

Had we done what we did only because we were drunk?

Would I take it back now that I was sober?

I knew the answers to those questions, and yet still, panic was flittering through me like a thousand angry wasps, muddling my words and making it impossible for me to see straight.

"It's fine, Eliza," River said, and this time, his voice was more subdued. His eyes met mine only briefly before he tugged on his hat, his gloves. He paused, opening his mouth before he shut it again, and then he just shook his head and walked out the door.

He had to give it a hard shove with his shoulder, clearing the bit of snow that had been blown over the porch despite the roof that hung over it. But once he made it out, he closed the door behind him, leaving me in the wake of the cold air that had rushed in.

I pulled the sheet tighter around me, staring at the door for a long moment before I looked down at Moose who was whimpering softly at my feet.

"It's okay, boy," I said, bending to pet behind his ear.

I just wished I believed my own words.

See You Never

River spent the morning shoveling snow, and I spent it trying to figure out what the hell was wrong with me.

I made a pot of coffee, and considered taking him a Thermos of it, but knew by the way he was heaving snow that he wouldn't take it. The same way I was sitting with my thoughts to try to work through them, he was working through his own by grunting and sweating and making his back ache.

So, I watched him from the window, holding my coffee between my hands more for warmth than to actually drink. And all the while, I stared at that boy, that man, the one I'd never expected to run into.

The one I'd run away *from*.

Nothing made sense. Finally, after years of wondering why he didn't ask me to stay, why he didn't come with me, why he didn't fight for me at *all*, I knew the reason why.

And somehow, it made me hurt even more than when I didn't know at all.

I was angry with him for not telling me, for stripping away my choice of what to do, had I known all the facts.

And I was thankful to him — for loving me enough to let me go, to shield me from the truth because he wanted my happiness more than his own.

And I was sad. *God*, I was so soul-crushingly sad. I was sad for the loss he had to endure on his own, for the years we'd lost that we could have been together, for the choice he had to make.

For the lack of choice he gave me.

I had plans. I had four weeks in Greece, and then a job on a river cruise in Austria, and then a three-month hiking trip along the southwest coast of the United Kingdom.

I had a new life now, and whether River had good intentions when he set me about it or not, he had chosen not to be a part of it. And now... now he wanted me to... to *what*?

I was only supposed to make a pit stop in Wellhaven.

I was only supposed to be here long enough to hug my family and have a little pie.

I was *not* supposed to get stuck in a cabin with my ex-husband, and I was certainly not supposed to sleep with him.

He'd ruined everything.

And now, I had a new longing in my gut, one I hadn't felt in so long that I truly thought I was over him. Over us.

But had I really ever lost it?

Or was I just trying to deny its existence, to pretend I was okay for the sake of moving on?

My thoughts whirled in a vicious storm all morning like that, tossing me in waves between anger and sorrow until I felt nothing but washed up and shredded.

River dragged himself inside somewhere around one, shaking the snow off him as best he could on the porch before he came inside. A little trail of cigarette smoke followed him in, and he stripped off his hat and coat, hanging them by the fire before his gaze finally found me.

"Sidewalk's clear, and I dug your car out, too. Skidder just came through with his snowplow.

It's not as big or as good as the city ones, but it'll be a while before they make it out here." River looked out the window. "Anyway, he's got some crew coming behind him with sand to try to keep the roads drivable, at least for a while. So, you should be good to go."

His eyes met mine briefly, and then he stalked over to the kitchen, pouring himself a finger of whiskey and throwing it back.

My rib cage shrank three sizes, the pressure so vicious on my lungs that I nearly keeled over. But instead, I crossed my arms over my chest to soothe it as much as I could, walking into the kitchen and leaning a hip against the counter.

I don't want to go.

I can't stay.

Last night didn't mean anything.

Last night meant everything.

I don't know what to do.

Please, tell me what to do.

"River..." I said, and he braced his hands on the counter before looking sideways at where I stood.

His eyes were bloodshot and glossy, and just one look from him stole any words I might have had forming.

"Come on," he said, standing. "You get your coat. I'll get your bag."

I hated how silent we were as I packed up what little I'd taken out of my bag, mostly toiletries and the clothes we'd littered the floor with last night. I hated even more the way Moose whimpered at my feet when I was pulling on my coat, as if he knew that I was leaving.

As if he knew that this time, I wasn't coming back.

"I love you, Moosey boy," I said, kneeling down to put my forehead against his. He licked at my face when I gave him a kiss, and I fought back the tears when I stood again. "You be good."

River had his hands in his pockets, but he withdrew them once I'd said my goodbyes to Moose, grabbing my suitcase. We walked outside in silence, and he helped me get my bag into the rental, and then we stood there by the driver door.

"Thank you," I finally managed. "For taking me in. I..." I smiled, trying to lighten things. "I hope I wasn't too much of a pest."

River winced at my words, shaking his head and looking down the road as he swallowed. "I'm going to follow you," he said. "Just to make sure you make it alright."

"You don't have to do that."

"I know."

I tried again for a joke. "You know, if you had a phone, I could just text you and let you know I'd made it."

He tried to smile, but it fell flat. "Alright, well. Take care, Eliza," he said, and then he turned his back on me before I had the chance to say anything in return.

I stood there and watched him go, watched him hop into his truck and fire the engine to life, letting it idle as he waited for me to get in and lead the way. My chest was on fire, tears pricking my eyes. I'd already said goodbye to that man once.

I never imagined I'd have to do it again.

I never imagined it'd hurt worse the second time around.

Before a single tear could fall, I slipped into my car, the engine groaning a little as I fired it up. As I checked my mirrors, my eyes caught River's in the rearview.

Just forty-eight hours ago, I knew exactly who I was.

I knew what my plan was, where my life was leading, what I'd see and do and explore next.

I knew where I'd been, and most importantly, I knew where I was going.

But then a blizzard had blown in unexpectedly, flipping everything upside down.

And now, I felt more lost than ever before.

Home is Where the Pie Is

All month long, I'd dreamed of the pumpkin pie that now sat on a beautiful, gold-trimmed china saucer in my lap.

When I was in New Zealand, I told the Kiwis I worked with about this pie. I described the cinnamon, the nutmeg, the creamy, delectable pumpkin and perfect buttery crust, salivating as I did so. My stomach grumbled at the thought of it on the very long flight back to the States. As I drove here from the airport, and all the time I was at River's, this pie was all I could think about.

Home is where Mama's pumpkin pie is, I thought.

And yet now that I had it within reach, just a fork sweep away from it being in my mouth, I couldn't eat it.

I pushed it around on my plate, eyes following the orangey brown smear of the filling. It smelled amazing, and I'd topped it with a heaping serving of Cool Whip. But still, I couldn't take even one bite.

I'd never felt this nauseous in my life.

I wished it was because I was still hungover, that the Advil and hangover cure River had given me hadn't worked. But the truth was that physically, I was fine.

But emotionally? Mentally?

I was a hot, steaming pile of garbage.

The surprise I'd looked forward to went off without a hitch, Mom and Dad both crying when they found me on the other side of the front door I'd knocked on. River had already pulled away after following me home by the time they ushered me inside, and from there, it was Mom fussing over whether there would be enough food or not, Grandma pinching my hips and saying I needed at least two servings before I withered away, Dad hugging me and doting on me, and my sister teasing me about how I had wrinkles now.

There was Christmas music and all the food I'd been lusting after. There was a warm fire and all the people I loved.

And yet, I was miserable.

"Mom's gonna be offended if you don't eat at least half of that," my sister, Beth, said from where she sat on the other end of the couch. Mom and Dad were in the kitchen with Grandma and Robert, Beth's husband, and Beth and I had retreated into the living room, sitting on the sofa in front of the Christmas tree.

"Trust me, I'd love to eat it all," I said, stacking a bite up on my fork. "If only my stomach would allow it."

Beth frowned, setting her own finished plate aside before she turned toward me. She had to move slowly, and she shifted a bit before getting her legs comfortably under her, thanks to her protruding belly.

Her protruding belly that was housing a baby. My future nephew.

And she hadn't even told me.

Just like Mama hadn't told me about her hip replacement surgery last fall, and Daddy hadn't told me that he sold both our horses two years ago.

I was in a house with my family, and yet I realized I'd been so caught up in living my own life, in chasing my own adventure, that I completely missed out on what was happening here.

I felt like a stranger.

I might as well have been.

"Well, you going to talk to me about it, or just sit there playing with your food?"

I sighed, dragging my fork across the plate to remove the pie I'd stacked on it just to stack another one right after. "I don't know what there is to say. I told you what happened."

"You did. But you haven't told me how you *feel* about being stuck in a cabin for two days with your ex-husband." She glanced into the kitchen before lowering her voice. "Or *sleeping* with him."

My sister looked nothing like me. Where my hair was dark as sin and slick straight, hers was dirty blonde and made of big barrel-wave curls. I tanned where she burned, her eyes were blue, where mine were inky wells of black.

But we had the same nose, and the same smile, and the same blood running through our veins.

And right now, I hated that she could see right through me.

I frowned, still staring at my pie. "Why doesn't anyone tell me anything anymore?"

Beth didn't answer, and when I looked up at her, she was watching me with the same look you might give an old woman slowly forgetting her memory. It was pity and sympathy and love all wrapped into one.

I hated it.

"Mom didn't tell me about her surgery," I continued. "Dad didn't tell me about the horses. *You* didn't tell me you're freaking *pregnant*." I pointed to her belly, letting my hand fall against my thigh with a slap as I shook my head. "And not a single one of you told me about River's parents."

Beth looked down at where her fingers curled together in her lap.

"Well?" I urged.

"What do you want from us, Eliza?" she finally asked, shaking her head as her blue eyes found mine. "You never wanted me to talk about River. Any time I would in that first year that you were gone, you'd get angry and ask me to stop. You told me it hurt to talk about him. You told me you didn't want to know."

"Yes, I realize that," I conceded. "But come on, this is different."

"Well, how was I supposed to know what was okay to mention and what wasn't? What you'd want to know versus what you wouldn't?"

Beth let out a frustrated breath, glancing at the tree before she found me again.

"You left this town like you never wanted any piece of it ever again, Eliza. I was trying to abide by your wishes. I was trying to give you what you wanted."

What I wanted.

I laughed under my breath at that.

It seemed everyone was trying to figure out what I wanted, including myself.

I abandoned my pie on the coffee table, crossing my arms over my chest. "I'm just... I feel like a fish out of water. I'm back home in the town I grew up in, and everything is the same, yet nothing is. River's parents are *gone*, Beth. They're gone. I never got to say goodbye. I never got to tell them how much they both meant to me. I never got to..." I held back the sob building in my throat, shaking my head. "I wasn't here for River. I wasn't here to help him, to listen to him, to hold his hand at the funeral. He went through all of that alone."

Beth's brows bent together, and she scooted close enough on the couch to where she could place her small, pale hand over mine.

"And he knew," I whispered, shaking my head as my eyes welled up. "He knew his dad was sick, that he wouldn't be here long. But he didn't tell me."

"Of course, he didn't," Beth said, as if it were obvious. "He loved you. He wanted you to be happy, and you had literally told him that you weren't happy here. Why would he try to keep you in that situation?"

"But it wasn't that simple," I said, frustrated. "We had been stuck in a rut for a full year. He was miserable, trying to work all those odds and ends jobs, breaking his back, never having a vacation or even a full weekend off. I was working at the supermarket. We were working, day in and day out, all day and night long sometimes just to pay our freaking bills." I shook my head. "That's not living, Beth. Neither one of us was living."

"I know," she said, rubbing her belly. I knew she was thinking about Robert, about how hard he worked to make ends meet, and how hard she worked to keep their little home up. "But then again, that may not be living to you, but to some of us, just getting by is enough. You know? I mean, sure, Robert and I don't have a bunch of nice things. We don't get to go take all these fancy vacations. But at the end of a long day, we come home to each other. We love watching our TV shows together, and we love sitting out at the lake watching the sunset, or taking a long drive through the old winding roads." She shrugged, a soft smile on her lips. "Sometimes you gotta look past all the hard things you go through and look at all the little things you have to be thankful for. Like someone to hug you, someone to laugh with." She patted her belly. "Someone to make new life with."

I swallowed down the emotion still strangling me. "I guess some of us just want more."

"Maybe," she said, but her smile told me she thought otherwise. "But maybe some of us just get lost and think we know what we want when really, we have no idea."

I frowned.

"Why do you think you're so sick to your stomach right now, Eliza?" she asked. "Why do you think you can't eat, can't fathom trying to sleep? Something has changed. Something inside you woke up that you didn't even realize was there, soundly sleeping, all this time."

Beth moved even closer, taking both of my hands in hers and looking into my eyes earnestly.

"Let me ask you this, sis. When you left, you said you were off to find adventure," she said, accentuating the word like it was an epic tale itself. "You've been gone for four years now. You've seen *dozens* of different countries, hundreds of cities and towns and farms and lakes and rivers. You've spoken new languages, walked down new streets, met new people and maybe even found a new version of yourself, too. But tell me this... have you found what you're looking for yet?"

My heart thumped hard at the question, another searing zip of pain splitting my chest.

"Because if you haven't," she continued, a little shrug on her shoulders and knowing smile on her lips. "Maybe it's because you've been looking in the wrong places. Maybe it's because it's been right here, in the town that built you, all along."

I watched my baby sister like she was an angel, or a psychopath, or maybe a cross between the two. I blinked over and over, my frown deepening the longer silence passed between us.

And the more those words she'd spoken sank in, the more the emotion I'd tried to fight back all evening long surfaced.

"Oh God," I whispered, pulling my hands from hers to cover my mouth. I shook my head. "You're right. You're right, Beth. I... I felt so stuck, so suffocated, that it felt like the only way out was to leave. But all this time, I've been searching for this... this *feeling*. I thought I would know it when it came. I thought one day I'd find a place or a person and everything would just click together and suddenly, right then, I'd know I was where I was supposed to be."

Beth nodded, smoothing her thumb over my knee.

"And I did," I said, emotion warping my face before I found a smile, found my sister's gaze. "I *did* find that feeling. But it wasn't in Europe, or Asia, or on a mountaintop or on a beautiful, white sand beach." I shook my head. "It was in that boring, tiny cabin with no power, no technology, no fancy food or fancy views or fancy entertainment. It was in front of that fireplace, under that stupid old blanket," I said on a laugh that Beth joined me in. "With that stupid man and that stupid dog." I sniffed. "I had everything I needed in that moment. And I felt it in my soul."

It was a revelation. As the words tumbled out of my mouth, I felt them soaring through every inch of my body like a cool breeze on a hot summer day. I pressed my hand to my heart, feeling where it beat inside my rib cage, where it was breaking with another realization.

"But I ran away from it," I whispered. "I found what I'd been looking for all this time, right where I left it, and it was like finally finding it scared me more than searching for it had." I shook my head, looking at Beth. "I left him. *Again.*" A sniff. "I am so, so stupid."

"You're not," she insisted, squeezing my leg. "You were just lost, Eliza. And sometimes that can be easier than being found."

My stomach toppled over itself, urging me to do something, but I had no idea what.

"What do I do now?" I asked my sister hopelessly.

To which she responded with only a smile, and a kiss to my forehead as she stood and grabbed my plate off the table. "You eat this pie," she said, shrugging. "And then, you go home."

"Home..." I echoed, taking the plate from her.

She nodded, thumbing my chin. "Home."

Then, she left me, joining her husband and our parents and grandmother in the kitchen. I watched them from where I sat — their smiles and laughter, my dad's arm around Mom's shoulders and Robert's hand interlaced tightly with Beth's.

And I felt it again, the same thing I'd felt coursing through me in the cabin with River.

Home.

It'd taken me too long to realize it. It'd caused pain to so many people I loved just for me to pull my head out of my ass and realize that what mattered most to me in my life wasn't what museums I'd been to or what continents I'd set foot on.

It was these people, right here in this tiny little map dot town that had a thousand others just like it sprawling across the United States, across the *world*.

I didn't need another plane, or boat, or train. I didn't need another beach, or city, or mountaintop.

What I needed was River.

I just hoped he needed me, too.

Merry Christmas, Baby

Knock-knock-knock.

My hands were shaking inside my gloves as I waited on River's doorstep, Moose barking like crazy on the other side. There was a warm glow coming from the windows, smoke from the chimney, and looking now at the cabin from the outside in only made me long for what I'd had inside it even more.

There was a low, grumbly command for Moose to be quiet, and then the door swung open, and River stood there on the other side of it.

It wasn't surprise or joy that passed over his face at the sight of me. Instead, it was a sort of indifference that made my heart sink. His jaw ticked, eyes taking me in before he swallowed. Moose was jumping around behind him, wagging his tail and trying not to bolt between his legs and the door to get to me.

"Hi," I whispered.

He didn't say a word, just watched me with those furrowed brows, his jaw set.

"Mind if I come in?" I asked, holding up the box in my hand. It was wrapped in a metallic green paper Mom had left over and topped with a simple red bow. "It's kinda cold out here."

River stood there a moment longer before he moved aside, allowing enough space for me to step through. As soon as I did, Moose was jumping on me, and I held the present out of the way just in time to save it from being mauled by his paws.

I chuckled, patting his paws where they landed on my chest before I kissed his wet nose. "Hey, boy. Missed you, too."

Moose was still whining softly when River finally got him down off me, and then we stood there in the entryway, me still wrapped in my coat and hat and gloves and scarf because the way River was watching me, I wasn't sure if I was invited to take them off and stay a while.

Well, here goes nothing...

"Merry Christmas," I said sheepishly, holding the box in my hand toward him.

River looked at it, looked at me, back at the box like it was a trap, and then back at me. "What are you doing here, Eliza?"

"Please," I begged, pushing the box closer to him. "Just open it."

He sighed, unfolding his arms where they were crossed over his chest and taking the box from my hands. He tore the paper open unceremoniously, ripping the ribbon off and letting it all fall to the ground. Then, he popped the lid on the small, rectangular box.

When it was open, he stilled.

For a long time, he just stared at that notebook, the one I'd carried with me all these years. It was thick and hardback, with a beautiful, matte black-and-white photograph of a rushing river winding between thick forests of trees, snow-topped mountains waiting, stretching up into the overcast sky in the background.

River swallowed, touching the cover before his eyes flicked to mine.

"Open it," I whispered.

He pulled it out of the box slowly, carefully, letting the box drop to the floor where the wrapping paper waited for it. Then, he balanced the book carefully in his hands and opened it to the first entry.

I watched his eyes scan the page, left to right over each sentence until he turned the page to the next one. He frowned more and more as he read, and my heart thumped loud and heavy in my ears.

"It's a journal," I explained. "Or a love letter. Maybe a cross between the two." I folded my hands together in front of me to keep myself from fidgeting. "I picked it up at the airport the day I left Vermont. And I've been writing in it every week since I left." I swallowed. "I've been writing it to you. *For* you."

River's eyes bounced over the pages as he turned them, and then they found mine, confusion written within the green depths.

That journal was one I'd written in religiously, and every entry started with *My Dearest River.*

I wrote to him about my travels, about the places I saw, the people I met. I shared the worst of weeks and the best of ones, too. I tried to explain the way I'd felt when I walked the streets of London, and the color of the sky as the sun set over Tuscany. I tried to imagine what he would have thought or felt if he were there with me.

I tried to write him into the story.

River turned another page, fingers tracing over the ink inside.

"I never stopped thinking of you," I said softly. "I always wished you were with me, and all along, I knew that something was missing."

River swallowed, nose flaring as he turned another page.

"I think I went looking for adventure, but what I didn't realize was that I left the best one behind."

At that, he stopped turning the pages, holding the book open in his hands and looking at me, instead. His eyes flicked back and forth between mine, and when a sheen of gloss covered them, emotion stole my next breath, tears building in my own eyes.

"You are my adventure, River," I whispered helplessly, two tears streaming simultaneously down each of my cheeks at the admission. "Just as much as you are my home."

I didn't miss the quiver of his bottom lip where he kept it buckled, or the way his next breath shuddered a bit with the effort to bring new oxygen into his lungs.

And I just shrugged, knowing there was no other way to put it. "I am lost without you."

As soon as the words left my lips, River blindly placed the journal on the kitchen counter behind him. Then, he swooped me into his arms, and I lost it.

I clung to him like life itself, wrapping my arms around his neck as his wound around my waist. He crushed me to him, and I tried to pull him closer still, sobbing into his shoulder.

"I don't care if it's in a big city or in another country or right here in this town we grew up in," I said through my tears. "I want this. I want you. I'll go wherever you want or stay right here in this tiny little cabin, as long as I can have you."

River framed my face, shaking his head before he kissed me hard and promising. Both of our faces were bent in agony, like that kiss killed us as much as it brought back every ounce of life we'd been missing.

"I thought I lost you again," he said, his words shaky and strained.

I clung to him tighter. "Oh, baby. You never lost me at all."

He shook his head, like he still couldn't believe I was there in his arms, before he met me with another long, deep kiss. Then, he was helping me strip out of my coat, my scarf, my hat and gloves and boots. He took me in his arms as soon as I was rid of my outerwear, and then he pulled me into his lap on the couch, surrounding me with his arms, his kisses, his love.

For a long while, we sat there just like that, holding each other and kissing and crying and not saying a single word. My heart surged with relief. My soul cried out in victory at finally being found. Every molecule of who I was came to life with that man by my side.

"Maybe you can have both," River said softly, when my cheeks were rosy and flushed from kissing.

"Both?"

"Me, and adventure."

I smiled, tapping his chest with my palm. "You *are* my adventure, silly. Weren't you listening?"

His eyes gleamed in the firelight as they searched mine. "Let's go, Eliza."

"Go?" I frowned.

"Let's do one more year out in the big wide world," he said. "But this time, we do it together."

My lips parted. "I... what are you saying?"

"One year. One year of going, doing, seeing. One year of exploring together. Then, we can decide what we want, where we want to settle — *if* we want to settle at all." He shook his head. "When you left, I let you go. I chose to stay here with my father, and I don't..." River swallowed. "I don't know that I regret that choice, because I loved those last months I had with my father. With my mother."

I squeezed him where I held him, letting him know I was there.

"But I lost you in the process. And now that I have you again, now that I know you were always mine just as I was always yours... I don't want to make another mistake. So, let's go. Let's see it all before we make a decision about what happens next."

My heart swelled. "You really mean it?"

"Yeah," River said on a nod. "Yeah, I really do. I want you, Eliza," he whispered, sliding his hand back over my cheek, fingers tangling in my hair. "And I want you to have your adventure, too."

I leaned into his palm, closing my eyes on a long breath before I kissed his warm skin, thinking over the life we'd already lived together, all the things we'd been through. "I think I've already had it."

But River shook his head, pulling me closer and whispering his own declaration over my lips before he kissed them, long and sweet.

"I think it's only just begun."

Moose hopped up onto the couch, practically right on top of us until we wiggled to make room for him, too. I laughed, kissing his head and rubbing behind his ears.

Then, River reached behind me, where the Christmas Blanket was hanging over the back of the couch. He smiled at me as he unfolded it, spreading it across the three of us, and then he took me and Moose both into his arms, holding us there by the fire.

When he gave me that blanket, he made a promise — that he would never stop fighting for us.

I knew as I held him in front of that fire, as he ran his hands through my hair and kissed my forehead softly, that his promise was true.

And that I would never stop fighting for us, either.

My heart fluttered, a smile spreading on my lips as I wrapped us up tighter in the blanket that brought me back to who I'd always been. I wished I'd never lost sight of that girl in the first place, but perhaps it made it sweeter now, knowing she was always there all along, knowing that River knew that, too, and that he believed I'd come back to him, just as I believed he'd never leave me, no matter how far away I went.

"Merry Christmas, baby," River whispered.

And I smiled, and held him closer, and thanked God for blizzards. "Merry Christmas."

The End

A Note to the Reader

Thank you for reading *The Christmas Blanket*! I wrote this little story because it was what my soul was craving this holiday season. I wanted to feel warm and cozy and hopeful, to wrap myself up in everything powerful and all-consuming about love. I hope you felt that, too.

If you're new to me and my books, I love to keep in touch with my readers. So, if you want to stay in touch, too, you can...

Sign up for my newsletter
(http://www.kandisteiner.com/newsletter)
Follow me on Instagram
(http://www.instagram.com/kandisteiner)
Join my reader group on Facebook
(http://www.facebook.com/
groups/kandilandks)

And if you liked *The Christmas Blanket,* you'll love my Becker Brothers series – free with Kindle

Unlimited! It follows four brothers finding love in a small Tennessee town, and trying to solve the mystery of their father's death along the way. Start with book one, On the Rocks (http://www.amazon.com/gp/product/B07T255NZ4/ref=as_li_tl?ie=UTF8&tag=ksreads-20&camp=1789&creative=9325&linkCode=as2&creativeASIN=B07T255NZ4&linkId=600378d0ebb57ae17689a4fe7cf24a24).

Or, if you'd rather a sports romance, I'm a huge football gal and this is my favorite season of the year. I've got two football books that you'll love if you're an NFL fan like me. Start with *The Wrong Game* (http://amzn.to/2ylJpPc), free with Kindle Unlimited!

All My Love,
Kandi

More from Kandi Steiner

The Becker Brothers Series
On the Rocks (book 1)
Neat (book 2)
Manhattan (book 3)
Old Fashioned (book 4)
Four brothers finding love in a small Tennessee town that revolves around a whiskey distillery with a dark past — including the mysterious death of their father.

The Best Kept Secrets Series
What He Doesn't Know (book 1)
What He Always Knew (book 2)
What He Never Knew (book 3)
Charlie's marriage is dying. She's perfectly content to go down in the flames, until her first love shows back up and reminds her the other way love can burn.

Make Me Hate You
Jasmine has been avoiding her best friend's

brother for years, but when they're both in the same house for a wedding, she can't resist him — no matter how she tries.

The Wrong Game
Gemma's plan is simple: invite a new guy to each home game using her season tickets for the Chicago Bears. It's the perfect way to avoid getting emotionally attached and also get some action. But after Zach gets his chance to be her practice round, he decides one game just isn't enough. A sexy, fun sports romance.

The Right Player
She's avoiding love at all costs. He wants nothing more than to lock her down. Sexy, hilarious and swoon-worthy, The Right Player is the perfect read for football season!

On the Way to You
It was only supposed to be a road trip, but when Cooper discovers the journal of the boy driving the getaway car, everything changes. An emotional, angsty road trip romance.

A Love Letter to Whiskey
An angsty, emotional romance between two lovers fighting the curse of bad timing.

Weightless
Young Natalie finds self-love and romance with her personal trainer, along with a slew of secrets that tie them together in ways she never thought possible.

Revelry
Recently divorced, Wren searches for clarity in a summer cabin outside of Seattle, where she makes an unforgettable connection with the broody, small town recluse next door.

Black Number Four
A college, Greek-life romance of a hot young poker star and the boy sent to take her down.

The Palm South University Series
Rush (http://www.kandisteiner.com/ newsletter) (book 1) FREE if you sign up for my newsletter!
Anchor, PSU #2
Pledge, PSU #3

Legacy, PSU #4

#1 NYT Bestselling Author Rachel Van Dyken says, "If Gossip Girl and Riverdale had a love child, it would be PSU." This angsty college series will be your next guilty addiction.

Tag Chaser

She made a bet that she could stop chasing military men, which seemed easy — until her knight in shining armor and latest client at work showed up in Army ACUs.

Song Chaser

Tanner and Kellee are perfect for each other. They frequent the same bars, love the same music, and have the same desire to rip each other's clothes off. Only problem? Tanner is still in love with his best friend.

About the Author

Kandi Steiner is a bestselling author and whiskey connoisseur living in Tampa, FL. Best known for writing "emotional rollercoaster" stories, she loves bringing flawed characters to life and writing about real, raw romance — in all its forms. No two Kandi Steiner books are the same, and if you're a lover of angsty, emotional, and inspirational reads, she's your gal.

An alumna of the University of Central Florida, Kandi graduated with a double major in Creative Writing and Advertising/PR with a minor in

Women's Studies. She started writing back in the 4th grade after reading the first Harry Potter installment. In 6th grade, she wrote and edited her own newspaper and distributed to her classmates. Eventually, the principal caught on and the newspaper was quickly halted, though Kandi tried fighting for her "freedom of press." She took particular interest in writing romance after college, as she has always been a die hard hopeless romantic, and likes to highlight all the challenges of love as well as the triumphs.

When Kandi isn't writing, you can find her reading books of all kinds, talking with her extremely vocal cat, and spending time with her friends and family. She enjoys live music, traveling, hiking, anything heavy in carbs, beach days, movie marathons, craft beer and sweet wine — not necessarily in that order.

CONNECT WITH KANDI:

NEWSLETTER
(http://www.kandisteiner.com/newsletter)
INSTAGRAM
(http://nstagram.com/kandisteiner)

FACEBOOK
(http://facebook.com/kandisteiner)
FACEBOOK READER GROUP
(http://www.facebook.com/groups/
kandilandks) (Kandiland)
GOODREADS
(https://www.goodreads.com/author/
show/7319216.Kandi_Steiner)
BOOKBUB
(http://bookbub.com/authors/kandi-steiner)
TWITTER
(http://twitter.com/kandisteiner)
WEBSITE
(http://www.kandisteiner.com/)

Kandi Steiner may be coming to a city near you!
Check out her "events" tab to see all the signings
she's attending in the near future.

SEE UPCOMING EVENTS
(http://www.kandisteiner.com/events)